that paints the

ning clouds that

then the whole

—*Dante*

Dreaming of Tuscany

Dreaming of Tuscany

Where to Find the Best There Is

Perfect Hilltowns • Splendid Palazzos • Rustic Farmhouses • Glorious Gardens • Authentic Cuisine
Great Wines • Intriguing Shops • Astounding Art • Luxurious Hotels • Hidden Discoveries

Barbara Milo Ohrbach

Photographs by Simon Upton

Additional photographs by Mel Ohrbach

RIZZOLI
NEW YORK

First Published in the United States of America in 2006 by
Rizzoli International Publications, Inc.
300 Park Avenue South, New York, NY 10010
www.rizzoliusa.com

2006 2007 2008 2009 / 10 9 8 7 6 5 4 3 2 1

Designed by Noël Claro   Map of Tuscany by Lonnie Sue Johnson
Printed in China

ISBN-13: 978-0-8478-2856-2   ISBN-10: 0-8478-2856-5
Library of Congress Control Number: 2006924887

The verse on the front endpaper is from *The Divine Comedy, Paradiso*, Canto XXVII, c. 1304–1321 by Dante Alighieri.
The passage on the back endpaper is from *The Italians*, 1964 by Luigi Barzini.

Also by Barbara Milo Ohrbach

The Scented Room

The Scented Room Gardening Notebook

Antiques at Home

Simply Flowers

A Token of Friendship

Memories of Childhood

A Bouquet of Flowers

A Cheerful Heart

The Spirit of America

Merry Christmas

Happy Birthday

All Things Are Possible . . . Pass the Word

Food for the Soul

Tabletops

If You Think You Can . . . You Can

Roses for the Scented Room

A Token of Love

Love Your Life

You're the Best

A Passion for Antiques

Grazie Infinite

George Bernard Shaw once famously said, "Married people should never travel together." I have to disagree, because this book would never have become a reality without my husband and longtime travel companion Mel Ohrbach, who contributed so much. He charmed every Tuscan we met with his impeccable Italian, happily drove from one end of the region to the other, loaded the car without complaining, unloaded the car without complaining, took pictures, labored over every word with me, and by being *molto simpatico* made what would have been a nearly impossible and very arduous project into an unforgettable adventure.

I am especially grateful to the many marvelous people who love Italy as much as I do and made *Dreaming of Tuscany* such a rewarding experience: my outstanding agents, Deborah Geltman and Gayle Benderoff, constant supporters who never wavered in their belief in this project; my photographer, Simon Upton, who took the most beautiful pictures with easygoing grace and humor—and has the most incredible sense of direction, and Karen Howes for keeping everything organized; my designer, Noël Claro; and my editor, Kathleen Jayes, who was a joy to work with, as was everyone on the Rizzoli team, especially Charles Miers, Ellen Nidy, and Jacob Lehman. A special thank-you to our Venetian friends Francesca Bortolotto Possati, Patrizia Serpe Piva, and Antonella Fontana for their hospitality en route.

Friends call me Sherlock Holmes because I love discovering the unexpected and the arcane when I'm traveling. But working on this book wouldn't have been the same without the wonderful recommendations, tips, and helpful advice from the following Doctor Watsons who always pointed me in the right direction: Elena Ricci Paracciani Bergamini, Simonetta Brandolini D'Adda, Patrizia Brughera, Marcella Cagnoli, Albiera Antinori, Consuelo Crespi, Christina Caughlin, Maddine Insalaco, Barrie Kerper, Rachel Newman, Ginevra Niccolini di Camugliano, Marjorie Shaw, Laurie Werner, Monica Willis, and my good friends Patti McCarthy, Jeanne Dimore, Renee Nahas, and Beth Allen.

It was a joy to wake up every morning in enchanting Tuscany to such beauty and know that we were going to photograph or experience something wonderful. The gracious people listed below generously shared their homes, treasures, hospitality, and interests with me. It was both a pleasure and a privilege—*grazie alla vostra gentilezza* to each and every one of them: Marchese Piero and Marchesa Francesca Antinori, and Albiera, Allegra, and Alessia Antinori, Dottore Fabio Guarducci, Paola Betticcini, Marcello Crini, Matia Barciulli, Cinzia Ninci, Mario Peccianti and Luciano Pietrapertosa, Marchesa Cristina Pucci, Laudomia Pucci, Lucy Tasca, Sabine Pretsch, Marchesi de'Frescobaldi: Rosaria, Bona, Tiziana and Diana Frescobaldi, and Maria Frescobaldi Benini, Piero Castellini, Paola Orsi, Alain Ducasse, Sarah Mompeurt, Robin Isley, Rachele Belladelli, Christolphe Martin, Filippo and Ginevra Niccolini di Camugliano, Lorenza de'Medici, Emanuela, Paolo, Roberto, and Guido Stucchi-Prinetti, Francesco Torre, Massimo Ferragamo, Victoria Hennessy, Marchese Giuseppe Ricci Paracciani Bergamini, Principessa Eleonora Massimo, Elena Ricci Paracciani Bergamini, Claudine Lechner, Simona Coltellini, Contessa Pannocchieschi d'Elci, Giuliangela Lops, Contessa Simonetta Brandolini D'Adda, Dottore Claudio Caprotti, Benedetta and Donata Origo, Dottore Luigi Zalum, Marily Young, Professore Gianfranco Fineschi, Katharina Alles Trauttmansdorff, Tanja Star-Busmann, Maddine Insalaco, Joe Vinson, Rachel Newman, Umberto Fenzi, Federica Manzieri, Benedetta Vitali, Faith Willinger, Jennifer Schwartz, Lorenzo Villoresi, Ilaria Guasco, Franco Torrini, Raffaela and Stefania Pagliai, Bona Tondinelli, Chiara Curradi, Vincenzo Fiorini, Rosellina Piccone, Gianfranco Pampaloni, Anna Carbone, Mauro Ciai, Paola and Giovanna Locchi, Laura Raffi, Dominique Nepi, Paola Simonelli, Benedetta Dalla Villa and Francesco Russo, Maria Paola Pedetta, Silvia and David Matassini, Vanessa Giovanelli, Enrico Costa, Kay Hawley-Brumley, Liugi Zaccardi, Clara Forlai, Silvia Kummer, Danytza Contreras, Francesca Gavoni, Davide Bertilaccio, Daniela Schmitz, Lou Hammond Associates, Mark Ricci, Christoph Dolz, and Silvia and Riccardo Baracchi. I would also like to thank the staff at IDI Travel, The Italian Trade Commission, the Italian Government Tourist Board, and Rail Europe.

Writing *Dreaming of Tuscany* was truly a dream. I had wanted to do this book for so long, never allowing myself to imagine that the reality would live up to my expectations. But it did—mainly because of the amazing Italian people I met on the journey. E. M. Forster said in *A Room with a View*, "Italians are born knowing the way.... Anyone can find places, but the finding of people is a gift from God." *Grazie di nuovo* to each and every one of them.

Table of Contents

Introduction

"Ama Ciò Che Fai"

(Love what you do)

Abbracci, baci, amore: hugs, kisses, love. Tuscany is a place you fall in love with at once. This book is about the Tuscany I love, and it's one I've been wanting to write for a long time. I've always had a wanderlust, and from the time I first visited Italy as a college student, it has drawn me back again and again.

As I was growing up I was determined to work in the fashion world, inspired by my grandmother who sewed exquisitely and worked for New York designer Jo Copeland. In my first job as a sportswear buyer, I decided I wanted to live in Italy and was transferred to the company's office in the regional capital of Florence. I fell even more in love with all things Tuscan. I was on a magic carpet, transported to a place that was glorious—finer and more appealing than I could ever imagine. When I returned to New York as vice president for Vogue Patterns, my job included covering the collections in Europe. The clothes in the glittering fashion shows, held in the opulent Pitti Palace's White Room, were luxurious and unforgettable.

The poet Anna Akhmatova said, "Italy is a dream that keeps returning for the rest of your life." And now, many years and many Italian trips later, my life has come full circle. I'm still as smitten as ever. My husband's love for the Italian language has led us to the rediscovery of long-lost Italian relatives and to many new adventures. Happily, Tuscany has become our second home. Our decades of traveling have fed our passion for the place, and now the wonderful opportunity to write this book is enabling me to share it with you.

One question I'm always asked when I make speeches throughout the country or write magazine articles is, "What are your favorite places?" As a seasoned, ever-curious traveler, I'm constantly adding to my voluminous files all the savvy details that answer this question. My sometimes scoffed-at lifelong habit of taking business cards from every place I've ever been and making copious notes has served me well.

Tuscans are optimistic and enjoy people. From the many (many, many) thoughtful townsfolk who patiently gave us directions when we got lost—the dreaded words *sempre diritto* (straight ahead) came up a lot—to the sophisticated, down-to-earth Tuscans, who took us under their wings and passed us from friend to friend in the kindest, most gracious manner—we were well looked-after. Our Italian friends, old and new, opened their hearts and address books, eagerly sharing their favorite secret discoveries. There's an old Italian joke that a secret is "telling just one person at a

PREVIOUS PAGE, LEFT: This famous view of the zigzag helix cypress trees planted by Iris and Antonio Origo at La Foce has become the symbol of the Val d'Orcia, and right, my favorite tote bag says "Florence".
RIGHT: Some of the many things I love about Tuscany include, clockwise, sumptuous tassels and trims from Florence's Antico Settificio; colorful signs offering good things to enjoy; magnificent gardens like this one at La Suvera near Siena.

SAY SMILE! A behind the scenes look at what can happen on photography—shooting outside all day in the rain. Above, photographer Simon Upton, my husband Mel and designer Piero Castellini with his adaptable horse.

time." In this case, it was me! And as a result I was able to peek through the keyhole of places most of us would never have the opportunity to see or even know about.

Italians, especially the Tuscans, have figured it all out. They enjoy a lifestyle that is cultured and stylish, simple and satisfying—after all, it is based on thousands of years of history. For them, the art of living is a balance of the sophisticated and the genuine in interior design, art, music, literature, architecture, craftsmanship, fashion, and of course, food and wine. What other country in the world could create a new political party called Il Partito della Bellezza, the "Party of Beauty." Begun in 2004 by MP Vittorio Sgarbi, its mission is to preserve "the extraordinary cultural identity of Italy, whose role—to be

beautiful—is a great gift that must not be squandered." As you wander through Tuscany you'll hear the word *bellissimo* again and again in everyday conversation. Beauty weaves through daily life like threads in a tapestry.

Dreaming of Tuscany is filled with beautiful photographs and insider information, a vade mecum on the true Tuscany. I've included all the recommendations I make to good friends—my carefully edited lists of our favorites, the best cooking schools, the finest craftsmen and workshops, the most elegant antiques shows, quirky regional antiques markets, verdant gardens open to the public, overflowing local food markets, and intriguing little-known museums—in addition to a selection of outstanding hotels, restaurants, all sorts of interesting shops, and more. Highlights include priceless advice from the pros on subjects like how to rent a villa and staying in an agriturismo, as well as famous chefs' suggestions on how to cook, eat, and drink like a Tuscan. There's also a chapter on how to keep on living like a Tuscan once you return home, which lists everything from furniture and olive oil to Italian seeds and terracotta pots for your garden.

Traveling in Tuscany, a region located in the center of lush Italy, is still a continuous journey of discovery even in a world that's increasingly homogenized, and crowded. All you have to do is turn off its main roads to find abundant surprises in the little towns that dot the countryside—word-of-mouth gems, hidden corners, and unexpected places that many tourists rarely encounter. In *Dreaming of Tuscany*, we've wandered off the beaten pathways to discover the out-of-the-ordinary—charming Renaissance villages with nary a person in sight, a tiny trattoria serving a meal you will always remember, or a linen shop with handwoven treasures unlike those you've ever seen before.

My aim in writing this book was not to be objective or all-encompassing; there are travel guides and the Internet for that. Instead it's a personal view of a place for which we have a great affection. We've traveled from one end of Tuscany to the other exploring, savoring, staying, eating, and shopping. Some were included because they are tried and true and we've enjoyed going to them for years, while others are new discoveries. We often intentionally left out the obvious in order to focus on the less well-known but infinitely more interesting. Included is our "best of the best," which is about quality, not status. Someone once said that "it is so hard to be simple." We're happy to report that the notion that "simplicity is the greatest luxury of all" still lives on in Tuscany.

I remember reading somewhere that former President Bill Clinton, in a speech he made in Europe some years ago, said, "When I just want to be happy, I go to Italy." This is the way many of us feel. Between the covers of this book are many fond memories of Tuscany: the smells—baking bread, harvested grapes, rich espresso, sweet lavender, basil and rosemary, ripe melons; the sounds—early morning chatter over the clatter of espresso cups, the tolling of the campanile bells, the echo of footsteps down empty ancient streets after lunch; the tastes—peppery olive oil, sweet tomatoes, spicy salumi, flaky *pecorino*, cool creamy gelato. As the Tuscans say, *"A tavola non s'invecchia."* (At the table, one never grows old). So come along with me on a blissful adventure and let me show you all the things I love in Tuscany, a place where you can expect to find smiling faces and where the sun almost always shines. *Andiamo!*

Barbara Milo Ohrbach
New York City
2006

Living in Style

Tuscan Interiors

*"What does it feel like to wake up in the
morning in a Tuscan farmhouse?"*

—Virginia Woolf

Virginia Woolf asked this question of the Marchesa Iris Origo—surely the right person. The marchesa had lived most of her fascinating and accomplished life in Tuscany, mainly at her estate La Foce, situated on 3,500 acres of Tuscan land that she and her husband Antonio worked hard to revitalize. It was there that she wrote critically acclaimed books such as *War in Val d'Orcia*, *The Merchant of Prato*, and *Images and Shadows* and created her world-famous garden, which is featured in the next chapter. So she knew the answer.

Although most of us are not brilliant writers looking for material, I do think that, like Woolf, we are curious about the way other people live. And of course the way of life in Tuscany has always been admired. Who wouldn't want to live in a rustic farmhouse surrounded by friends, family, good food, and wine in a country where the sun always seems to shine? In a sense you can't separate the home from the spirit of the people who live in it, and what we envy about the Italians is their ability to create harmonious beauty with seemingly effortless style. How do they do it?

Gae Aulenti, the distinguished architect,

OPENING PICTURE: The handsome salon at Palazzo Niccolini in Florence with its pastel frescoes, original cotto fiorentina floors, and antique family pieces.
OVERLEAF LEFT: Yards of fine muslin define this simple but luxurious bedroom and right, relaxing under the Tuscan sun.
THIS PAGE, LEFT: Bougainvillea grows in profusion on a hilltop Tuscan farmhouse near Montalcino.

has said that Italian taste is among the most refined in the world, derived from a tradition cultivated over the centuries. There's no place where this tradition is more apparent than in Tuscany. Here, people live their everyday lives surrounded by layers of history that go back thousands of years, mixing traditional antiquities with modern design.

City mansions or palaces (*palazzi*), castles (*castelli*), and country estates (*villas*) generally have grand proportions, spacious rooms, high ceilings, oversized fireplaces, thick walls, elegant painted frescoes, and marble floors—all indications of the original owners' stature and wealth. In these old houses the public rooms, such as the living, drawing, and sitting rooms and the music room or library, were always situated on the *piano nobile*, or first floor, with the kitchen below. Private rooms, such as bedrooms and baths, were on the floors above.

Their rooms are usually not self-consciously decorated, furnished with inherited antiques and furniture, often large pieces created just for these spaciously proportioned interiors. Modern design influences, for which Italy has become famous, are also part of the picture.

PREVIOUS PAGE, LEFT: Elegant frescoes in a luxurious red bedroom.
PREVIOUS PAGE, RIGHT: Back-lit glass shelves shimmer in a library designed by Roberto Monsani.
RIGHT: Vaulted ceilings and colorful fabrics define this restored farmhouse.
NEXT PAGE: Old paired with new at Palazzo Pucci.

Sleek leather sofas, steel lamps, molded plastic chairs, and accessories designed by familiar names such as Giò Ponte, Piero Fornasetti, Marco Zanuso, Franco Albini, and Ettore Sottsass add a sometimes unexpectedly avant-garde slant to ancient surroundings.

Henry James wrote in 1873: "I find I like fine old rooms that have been occupied in a fine old way." Today, Tuscans are living in these fine old rooms in new ways, adapting them to a more informal lifestyle and adding spas, entertainment areas, and home offices. Some large palazzi and country villas have been divided into smaller but no less elegant apartments, following the trend that began in England and France, making them more livable as well as very desirable places to live.

"Italians seem hardly able to look at a high place without longing to put something on

PREVIOUS PAGE, LEFT: An aerie designed by Gae Aulenti for Emilio and Cristina Pucci in 1968 includes a sleek stainless steel living room and bedroom.
PREVIOUS PAGE, RIGHT: Ikat gilt armchair, a still life with abstract paintings and stacks of antique porcelain.
ABOVE: A bedroom with twelfth-century wall painting, and right, mementos fill a red étagère.

top of it," said the nineteenth-century writer Samuel Butler. Nowhere is this statement better illustrated than on a drive through the verdant, rolling Tuscan countryside dotted with olive trees and orchards, where homes adorn every peak. The beauty of these structures—from elegant villas and castles to simple farmhouses and sensitively converted agricultural buildings—illustrates what we have come to think of as *la dolce vita*.

Lorenzo di Medici defined the term *"villegiatura,"* an escape from the city into the idyllic countryside, when he settled in the Tuscan hills during the sixteenth century, bringing with him the movers and shakers of

PREVIOUS PAGE: Rooms with a view: above left, the altana suite at Palazzo Niccolini overlooking the Duomo in Florence; below left, the Palazzo Pubblico in Siena seen from Palazzo d'Elci; right, a view of the Sienese hills.
THIS PAGE: Explore the lush Tuscan countryside!

Renaissance Florence. There at the Medici estates they discussed classical culture—painting, literature, sculpture, science, and music. To this day, many Tuscans enjoy primary (if not second) homes in the country. These rural retreats are a tradition that keeps them in touch with the land and a dependable supply of life's small, but important necessities, like wine, olive oil, and fresh flowers.

Such rural abodes are very much in step with their environment, utilizing local materials and ancient techniques where possible; and since in Italy most architects are interior designers—and most interior designers, architects—there's an obvious harmony between the structure of the house and its furnishing. Stylish designer Piero Castellini is a good example of someone who does both. His weekend home in Tuscany, an old, converted farmhouse, is filled with colorful fabrics, linens, and furniture from his home décor company.

The Tuscans are in a unique position of having been fortunate enough to sustain a tradition of artisans who have adapted, refined, and kept alive the old crafts,

PREVIOUS PAGE, LEFT: Piero Castellini before a morning ride, and right, a room in his farmhouse filled with elegant saddles and tack.
LEFT: Eighteenth-century engravings hang above a hand-painted nineteenth-century bureau.
RIGHT, ABOVE: An ancient sculpture amid family photos, and below, a Roman bust on a corner shelf.
NEXT PAGE, CLOCKWISE FROM LEFT: Dazzling Tuscan blues: Zuber wallpaper circa 1850; a Tuscan pottery scene; a graceful door; a lyre-back side chair.

LEFT AND ABOVE: Traditional Tuscan greens accent a farmhouse kitchen, left, and bedroom, above.
NEXT PAGE: The inviting pool at Fonte de'Medici.

employing them in all aspects of restoration and decoration. Woodcarving, marble crafts, stonecutting, historic fabric weaving, iron- and metalworking, and fresco painting are just some of the skills passed down from one generation to the next (see Chapter Four, which focuses on Tuscan talent and creativity, for a more in-depth look).

In the 1960s the Tuscan feudal system of farming (*mezzadria*), which had been in place since the eighteenth century, came to an end after the peasants, or *contadini*, abandoned their farms and migrated to the cities to take salaried jobs. Many of these humble farmhouses were then acquired by Italians— and foreigners—looking for country homes. These old stone *casa colonicas* were frequently

ABOVE: Pale tones of pink, blue, and green enhance delicate frescoes in a sitting room filled with dried flowers that complement the color scheme. A silver drinks tray completes the picture.

set on hills, with medieval examples featuring a central lookout tower, a necessity in those perilous times. The lower floor was critical to the farm's workings and contained storerooms for carts, grains, and farm equipment. Many also had stalls and stables for the valuable animals, and even a henhouse. It was a sensible arrangement, especially in winter, as the heat from the animals rose to warm the upper floor where the inhabitants lived. Usually reached by an outside staircase, the family congregated here in the large kitchen with its ovens. Often there was a loggia, or open air porch, on the south side of the building used for various purposes when the weather turned warm.

Today these farmhouses have been renovated in the most interesting ways. Large rooms have been created by removing walls and stalls, rustic wood beams have been

ABOVE: A modern painting by Carlo Pizzichini hangs on pale green hand-plastered walls.
NEXT PAGE: Italians love relaxing alfresco whether on a loggia, in a garden, or even in an orchard.

preserved and polished, terracotta floors replaced, and fireplaces refitted creating a contemporary environment with a nod to the past that is at once comfortable but still evocative. Lovely colors frequently are used in the chalky mixture of plaster and paint or in more complex techniques, such as *marmorino*, a combination of lime putty, marble powder, and pigment. Tints of lemon yellow, saffron, ochre, peach, or teal blue reflect the sunshine and make each room look even more alive.

Iris Origo's response to Virginia Woolf's question was: "Come and see." Haven't you ever dreamed of waking up in a Tuscan farmhouse? Or villa? Or palazzo? Or castle? If you have, this chapter should, I hope, whet your appetite and be a valuable guide the next time you decide to plan a trip to one of the prettiest places on earth.

One of the best (and nicest) ways to get to know Tuscany is to rent a property there. Having your own house gives you the opportunity to become a Tuscan, even if it's only for a short time—to visit the nearby food markets, sample the local wines and, best of all, buy all the fresh flowers you want. I wish we had had this list when we rented our first house in Tuscany many years ago. It was an adventure filled with unexpected surprises—some not as pleasant as others. To help you avoid the same pitfalls, I asked Contessa Simonetta Brandolini d'Adda, the founder with her husband of The Best in Italy, a company specializing in the rental of luxurious villas in Tuscany, to share her insider advice. Her company, based in Florence, is over twenty-five years old, and its great success is due to word-of-mouth recommendations based on high-quality properties and attention to detail. She really understands the preferences of Americans when they are renting abroad. After reading Simonetta's list, I find that she is even more particular than fussy me, and has tried to think of everything you might need to ensure that your fantasy of la dolce vita matches reality.

Selecting a Rental Company

Choosing the right rental company is essential. There are many, so make sure that the one you choose has been in business a substantial amount of time in Italy. The best specialize in personalized attention and can fill special requests.

• Be sure that the company has visited the property that you are considering renting. Many have not seen all of the homes in their listings and do not know important details about layouts, staff, and amenities.

• Someone should meet you upon arrival at the property to show you around. Ask whom you will coordinate with during your stay. This is a must.

• You may think Internet research is sufficient, but a reputable company should have printed materials and, more importantly, should communicate with you personally throughout the rental process up to your arrival.

Location

Decide what area of Tuscany you prefer to rent in. If you can't decide, ask for a recommendation from a friend who loves Italy, read travel literature, or look at a map to see what cities interest you most. Italy has a good train system, so you can easily rent in Tuscany and travel for the day to other intriguing places like Rome, Venice, or the cities in between, making your stay even more special.

Selecting Dates

The first time we rented a house in Tuscany, it was only for one week, which wasn't long enough. We had just gotten settled when it was time to leave. I recommend renting for at least two weeks, to savor the full flavor of living in the place. Many of the better rental companies rent for a minimum of two weeks, anyway.

• You must plan early. Top properties are often rented a year in advance, because many people reserve the same property (usually the most desirable ones) over and over again.

• Consider renting off-season. June and September are the busiest months. Early spring and late fall are less crowded, so there are more opportunities for obtaining the rental you want and relatively hassle-free touring.

• Most rentals in Italy start and end on a Saturday, which is important to know when making your travel arrangements, so be sure to check.

The Property

Make sure that you have photographs, a brochure, and a proper description of the villa, farmhouse, or apartment that you are renting. Find out how many bedrooms it has and if there are enough bathrooms for the comfort of the guests. The kitchen should be well appointed with china, flatware, pots and pans, etc. Ask about amenities like working fireplaces.

• Find out about outdoor areas. Are they equipped for dining and relaxing during the warm summer months? Is there a pool? Are there tennis courts? If so, is there staff to take care of them, and are they included in the rental?

• Be sure to determine if heating, air conditioning, electricity, and telephone are included or billed separately.

Staff

Enquire whether there is a full-time staff, and if so, how large. If not, is there someone who will come to clean? Do they know the property well?

• Ask about staff responsibilities: will they do the cleaning, grocery shopping, cooking, ironing, care for the grounds and pool, or anything else that you would expect them to do while you are there? This must be clear at the outset.

• Since your rental will probably start on a Saturday, and most stores are closed on Sunday, be sure that the basics, such as milk, bread, coffee, and juice will be in your refrigerator when you arrive.

Amenities

The following are some questions to ask before you rent:

• What type of mattresses are used?

• Are the bed linens natural fibers? Cotton? Linen? How often are they changed?

• Are there blankets and space heaters in case of a rare cool evening?

• Are there enough towels for bathrooms and for the pool, and how often are they replaced?

• What type of telephone service is provided? Is there an Internet connection?

• This is Italy, so find out if there may be electricity limitations—for example, can you use the dishwasher when the pool pump and other appliances are running?

• Is a washer/dryer available? Is there a laundry or drying room where clothes can be hung?

• Are there screens (a new trend) on the bedroom windows, or other techniques to keep mosquitoes out?

• The best rental companies provide a comprehensive book for each property that usually includes detailed notes on the house, language tips, emergency numbers, and invaluable information on local restaurants, wineries, nearby hill towns, day-trip suggestions, and even maps of how to get there. (Simonetta's are so well done that you hardly need any other guidebook). The insider tips in these guides will point you in the right direction immediately, enabling you to enjoy every moment of your day.

Contracts

Make sure your rental contract has a defined cancellation policy.

• Travel insurance is important and must be purchased before you leave.

• A security deposit is usually part of the contract, and any damage or breakage is usually deducted from this deposit. Find out exactly when the deposit will be returned to you.

Contessa Simonetta Brandolini d'Adda
The Best in Italy
Via Ugo Foscolo, 72
Florence 50124
T 011-39-055-223-064
F 011-39-055-229-8912
www.thebestinitaly.com
Email: thebestinitaly@thebestinitaly.com

ABOVE: The imposing entrance to one of the ancient palazzos sitting in the hills surrounding Florence that can be rented.

We recently rented an apartment in Florence, which was fun. It was on the Oltrarno, the other side of the Arno River, which gave us the opportunity to wander the narrow streets and passages of this older part of the city. We went to the food market in Santo Spirito most mornings and were able to bring home the freshest ingredients that we used to cook in our simple kitchen. You can rent a beautifully decorated apartment by the week or month from the following company:

Windows on Tuscany
Via de' Serragli, 6r
Florence 50124
T 011-39-055-268-510
F 011-39-055-238-1524
www.windowsontuscany.com
Email: info@windowsontuscany.com

If you yearn for a relaxed way to spend a Tuscan vacation and want to stay somewhere in the countryside, you might try an agriturismo. The term can sometimes be confusing to the foreign visitor. In Italy, it is a general category that can mean anything from a simple cottage or farmhouse to an apartment in a cluster of converted farm buildings or someone's ancestral castle. Accommodations range from basic to luxurious. Most are off the beaten path, located in enchanting hills in the midst of vineyards, olive trees, or orchards—an ideal spot for those seeking a rural getaway in harmony with nature. The majority are family-owned and operated.

The agriturismo came into existence for a very important reason. In the 1960s as European farm prices dropped, generations of struggling farmers whose families had tilled the land for centuries were faced with having to abandon their property for jobs in the cities. Countless farm buildings, ancient villages, and churches would have been destroyed by urban development if a move hadn't been made to protect these picturesque landscapes. As a solution, many European governments began to subsidize those farmers and property owners who agreed to take in tourists in return for preserving the land. This concept has been an immense success, especially in Italy; for example, in the province of Siena alone there are said to be more than three thousand agriturismos.

Today, the first thing that strikes you as you approach any Tuscan town is a signpost loaded with arrows painted with the name of each agriturismo in the area, all pointing in the general direction of their locations. It's almost impossible to know which one to choose.

To get some advice, I spoke with Albiera Antinori of the illustrious Antinori family, whose name has been associated for centuries with great wines and vineyards, and who has become an expert on the subject. In the wonderful Italian way, she and her two delightful sisters, Alessia and Allegra, are in the wine business together with their father, Marchese Piero Antinori, and under Albiera's direction they have opened a deluxe agriturismo. Called Fonte de'Medici, it is located a convenient thirty minutes south of Florence in the midst of one of their largest vineyards famous for its outstanding, award-winning wines (discussed in Chapter Three). Albiera is excited about this new venture, and her enthusiasm is contagious. Here she kindly shares some general tips on what you can expect from an agriturismo:

• Staying at an agriturismo should be approached as a rural experience, where most things are done in an informal style.

• It is not a hotel, but more like renting a house or an apartment. The decor is sometimes very casual and can even be spare. Consequently, the rates are usually more modest. Rentals are generally for a minimum of one week, in and out on Saturday afternoons.

• Most services are minimal, so don't expect to find your bed turned down every night or a concierge making your dinner reservations, as there is usually no daily maid service. It is sometimes possible to make arrangements for services you might require for a separate fee.

• As a rule, there is no restaurant; however, in true Tuscan fashion, friendly staff and owners will happily share their list of favorite neighborhood trattorias. This is sometimes one of the best things about traveling in Italy, because it leads to unexpected discoveries and wonderful meals in small places you would never have known about.

• You will normally have a kitchen, which means you can shop for fresh local produce in the markets and take advantage of dining alfresco on outdoor terraces.

∾ ∾ ∾ ∾ ∾ ∾

With so many agriturismos and such a wide range to choose from, you will need to do some research to find the one for you. Here we have included a small list of some of our favorites. Each is exceptional in its own way.

Fonte de'Medici

Via Santa Maria a Macerata, 31
50020 Montefiridolfi
011-39-055-824-4700
www.fontedemedici.com
mail@fontedemedici.com

In the fifteenth century travelers between Florence and Siena would rest and drink from a spring that still runs through what was the tiny medieval village of Santa Maria a Macerata. Today this cluster of stone buildings is at the heart of the Antinori family's luxurious Fonte de'Medici. When you arrive at reception, you are surrounded by manicured gardens. Off to the left is a large, handsome pool overlooking extraordinary views of the Tignanello vineyards with olive groves and in the distance the Elsa Valley. Pure heaven!

RIGHT: The sunny lemon yellow dining room of Osteria di Passignano awaits luncheon guests.

The complex is divided into two separate groups of large stone farm buildings, known in Italy as *poderi*. One, Podere Vivaio, is on the shore of nearby Lake Buca del Granchio. We had to drive through the vineyards to our apartment in the second, Podere Tignanello, really on top of the world. Tignanello consists of seven spacious and very elegant units. Smaller apartments are available in the main reception building.

The restoration of the farmhouses is impeccable and features burnished terracotta floors, large stone fireplaces, and loggias with their own outdoor grills, which means dining while enjoying beautiful views. A major effort was made to sensitively preserve the old buildings and interiors. Our two-bedroom apartment was originally the old chapel, and the focal point of the living room is the original altar. The kitchens are thoughtfully stocked with Antinori wines, and the bathrooms are large and modern. The apartments include central heating, television, telephones, and even an up-to-date security system. Obviously this is the top of the line for an agriturismo. If you are there in the spring or summer, the scent of thousands of lavender bushes, climbing roses, and bougainvillea is delightfully overwhelming!

Osteria di Passignano

Via Passignano, 33
50028 Tavarnelle Val di Pesa
www.osteriadipassignano.com
marcello.crini@tin.it
011-39-055-807-1278

One mile south of Fonte de'Medici is Badia a Passignano, a two-thousand-year-old abbey now owned by the Antinoris. You can make an appointment to visit the majestic monastery and its ancient wine cellars. And you should make a reservation to visit the restaurant, Osteria di Passignano, one of our favorites. Opened in 2000, it has become a destination restaurant in Tuscany, featuring no-nonsense classic regional cuisine made with the freshest local ingredients. Everything on the menu is delicious and simply but beautifully served. Our first experience here was sublime. Before our meal, we were served three different Tuscan olive oils, from mild to peppery, in small white porcelain ramekins. They arrived on a carved olive wood tray along with little pieces of freshly baked bread. It was a delicious introduction to what was to be a most memorable meal, which included seasonal mushroom soup with wild herb ravioli and pecorino cheeses with homemade marmalade, chutney, and honey. Of course, you will be

drinking the best Antinori wines. If you fall in love with one or two, stop in the shop on the way out and have your favorite shipped home.

Tenuta di Vico d'Arbia e Larniano

Strada di Pieve a Bozzone, 88
53100 Siena
Tel/Fax: 011-39-0577-369-193
www.vicodarbia.com
info@vicodarbia.com

If Siena is one of your favorite cities, you will enjoy staying in one of these four distinctive stone farmhouses located in the countryside just a ten-minute drive away. They have been beautifully restored by Sienese architect Giuliangela Lops and furnished with impeccable taste by the delightful owners. No expense has been spared, and no detail overlooked.

Each farmhouse is a little different, accommodating four to fourteen people. They all offer an overwhelming sense of comfort and provide everything you need—laundry rooms, fireplaces, satellite TVs, fax machines, and even DVDs. There are beautifully landscaped alfresco dining areas, and two of the houses have their own private swimming pools. The interior colors are harmonious, the linens creamy, the bathrooms large and modern, and the kitchens fully equipped with lovely china, glassware, and tableware. Antique accents are evident throughout—beautiful, big Tuscan pieces like heavy, carved wood sideboards that look original to each house. Anyone who enjoys decorating will love staying here. In fact, the place has been photographed by *Italian Architectural Digest* magazine.

La Foce

Strada della Vittoria, 61
53042 Chianciano Terme
011-39-0578-691-01
www.lafoce.com
info@lafoce.com

For anyone who has read early twentieth-century author Iris Origo's books, a stay in one of the fifteen centuries-old farmhouses on the sprawling La Foce estate will be a dream come true. Her daughters Donata and Benedetta Origo have meticulously restored and redecorated many of them in the nicest way, with a mixture of antique Tuscan country pieces accented with bright fabrics and hand-woven rugs. Everything has been sensibly thought out and anticipated, down to the details. While we were there, a family with four children was expected, and playpens and cribs were set up for them.

ABOVE: A typical Tuscan farmhouse with colorful shutters and flowers growing everywhere.

Each house has its own private pool and is in an unusually peaceful setting, with breathtaking views of Mount Amiata and the Val d'Orcia. The landscaping is impeccable; beautiful Mediterranean plants and flowers abound. Be sure to sign up for the guided tour of La Foce's exceptional formal gardens (see Chapter Two).

La Foce's location is almost perfect for exploring southern Tuscany and all the surrounding little hill towns (featured in Chapter Seven)—gems that have not yet been overly exploited by tourism. There are two magnificent abbeys close by—Sant'Antimo and Monte Oliveto Maggiore—that should not be missed. If you love music and art, visit in mid-summer when "Incontri in Terra di Siena," the exquisite chamber music festival founded by Benedetta Origo and her son Antonio Lysy, takes place along with art shows at Castelluccio, the medieval castle that is part of the estate.

If you are just starting to look for agriturismos or farmhouses to rent, there are many options open to you—almost too many. One option is to work with a consultant who has vetted the property already. Another is to begin by looking at some websites. There are too many to list all of them here, so we have included several just to get you started.

Trust and Travel

Katharina Allès Trauttmansdorff founded her company Trust and Travel in 1991 and is a consultant to many tasteful agriturismos. She is a trained architect who was involved with the restoration of the wonderful old guesthouses at La Foce. She lists a select group of farmhouses and agriturismos on her website.

Trust and Travel
Kaiserstrasse 41/2
1070 Vienna, Austria
011-43-1-522-4349
www.trustandtravel.com
or
15 rue Singer
75016, Paris
011-33-1-40-29-47-32

Italy Farm Holidays

Italy Farm Holidays is operated by Ralph and Susan Levey, who have more than twenty-eight years of experience traveling through the Italian countryside. They live in a farmhouse in Tuscany and specialize in helping sophisticated travelers choose the right accommodation, whether a farmhouse or villa. They visit and inspect every property shown on their website, many of which are located in the midst of vineyards and olive orchards.

Italy Farm Holidays
547 Martling Ave.
Tarrytown, NY 10591
914-631-7880
www.italyfarmholidays.com

One last note—here are three Italian websites translated into English:

www.agriturismo.it Provides a list of farmhouses and agriturismos within the provinces of Tuscany, and includes a photograph and description of each property.

www.chiantiferie.net A consortium of about twenty-five restored farmhouses and agriturismos between Florence and Siena. They have a printed catalog that includes photographs and descriptions of each property.

www.agriturismo.regione.toscana.it Features a list and descriptions of agriturismos in Tuscany.

TWO

Beyond the Gates

Inside Tuscan Gardens

"Why would you be anywhere else when you can be in Italy?"

—Edith Wharton

Edith Wharton loved Italy from the time she first traveled there as a child and was forever captivated by the glory and inspiration of the Old World. As a turn-of-the-century expatriate, she enthusiastically visited many important villas and gardens in Italy—especially those in Tuscany—often in the company of kindred spirits like art expert Bernhard Berenson, whose Villa I Tatti was almost a second home. In 1904 she wrote a book called *Italian Villas and Their Gardens*, which became a classic. It has influenced and inspired generations of gardeners (including me) and is still in print over one hundred years later.

Wharton's book opens with a chapter on the exquisite gardens and villas of Florence. In it she says that "the garden must be studied in relation to the house and both in relation to the landscape," and that "the old Italian garden was meant to be lived in," emphasizing the idea that the classic Renaissance garden was based on a rural lifestyle of a very civilized manner. The garden was an extension of the house, furnished with carved stone benches and tables and decorated with marble statues and sculptures.

Villegiatura, or the custom of urbane Italians enjoying a pleasant rural retreat in their country homes, is a notion that has been around since Roman times. Centuries later, in 1450, Florentine scholar Leon Battista Alberti

OPENING PICTURE: Palazzo Antinori's elegant garden. OVERLEAF LEFT: Topiary hedges are trimmed and, right, an ancient statue smiles at Villa Gamberaia. RIGHT: Cypresses frame the famous view in La Foce's garden, designed by Cecil Pinsent.

revived this concept with his treatise *De Re Aedificatoria*. His book heaped praise on the many attributes of country life in the villa and encouraged many to build country retreats away from the stifling summer heat and diseases of the towns. The book—and the idea—started a major trend. "Nature and architecture should be in harmony," he wrote, and the grand villas situated on hillsides in the midst of dusty olive groves and fragrant fruit orchards were designed not to overwhelm but to complement the gardens.

As a result, Renaissance estates became the center of social life outside the city. Prominent scholars, poets, writers, sculptors, architects, and artists (including Michelangelo) were guests of their patrons—the noble Medicis and their cultured and wealthy aristocratic friends—who congregated in these pleasurable rural places of serenity, introspection, and civilized activity. Most of the gardens we see today—in Tuscany as well as other parts of Italy, France, England, and even the United States—reflect these humanistic ideals of the Renaissance.

"The very air is full of architecture," said Edith Wharton, and indeed in most Tuscan gardens architectural elements form the basic structure and are the focal point of the garden—not flowers, not lawns, nor anything that could be normally taken for granted. Order and symmetry are all. A central axis usually intersects vast vistas

LEFT: An urn planted with delicate ivy geranium sits at the top of another garden room at La Foce. RIGHT: Stone figures like this alert dog, above, and chubby putto, below, decorate Tuscan gardens.

that are joined by allées of old brick walls or orderly rows of elegant cypress trees. The uneven Tuscan terrain often provided an excuse to build spectacular architectural structures: dramatic amphitheaters carved into hillsides or ornate, multilevel terraces with double staircases that guided visitors from one level to the next. Carved stone statues play a large part in the scheme—allegorical figures, poetical busts, vases, urns, and fanciful animals and sea creatures enliven niches, grottos, and the top of balustrades. Many of these gardens were designed by such prominent Renaissance architects as Michelozzo Michelozzi, Antonio Rossellino, Bernardo Buontalenti, and Baldassare Peruzzi.

If the stone elements are the bones, then the outdoor "garden rooms" are the heart of Tuscan gardens. Perfectly proportioned high brick walls and evergreen hedges create intimate spaces that flow into one another, providing undisturbed oases of sun and shade, scented by herb-filled parterres, graceful topiaries, potted lemon trees, tumbling roses, and fragrant jasmine. In some, you can still find a *giardino secreto*, or secret garden, a cool private refuge hidden away in a corner, a romantic idea revived from the Middle Ages.

If you are in Tuscany during the hot summer, you'll immediately understand why water is a focal point of the gardens. Ornamental pools sparkle in the Italian sun, and the cool rush of

LEFT: After a morning cooking and eating at Badia a Coltibuono, it's time to take a stroll in the relaxing Renaissance garden behind the abbey.

fountains and cascades adds a dimension of sound. Italians love little jokes, and the *giochi d'acqua* is one of them—concealed water jets attached to mechanical devices that are imbedded in steps, balustrades, and even paths. The seventeenth-century garden visitor would trip the mechanism (or a gleeful gardener would turn it on), resulting in shrieks of delight as everyone was unexpectedly sprayed. They are still working in the Villa Torrigiani (see listing), so beware.

The Italian sense of playfulness also lingers in the *romitorio* or hermitage. A small, charming building, or even a thatched hut, it was usually sited on a hill with views of the Tuscan countryside, and designed as if the imaginary hermit who lived there just stepped out for a moment. There were also mazes of tall privet, yew, or boxwood hedges, a Renaissance invention created to delight children—or, unintentionally, to shield amorous couples from their ever-present chaperones.

It wasn't until the seventeenth century that other design trends started to cast their influence on Tuscan gardens. The Baroque movement dictated gardens that were much more dramatic. Lavish displays and a more obvious sensibility take the place of the more contemplative Renaissance perspective. Later, in the nineteenth century, English garden design became the rage, and many old Tuscan gardens were remodeled to reflect the ideal of the period, including, for example, the ill-suited and ubiquitous herba-

ceous borders. Fortunately, many of the Anglo-American residents who came later—Sybil Cutting, Bernhard Berenson, and Janet Ross, to name a few—engaged garden architects such as Cecil Pinsent, who returned the gardens to the Italian Renaissance landscape designs. In fact, English writer George Sitwell noted in 1909, "If the world is to make great gardens again, we must both discover and apply in the changed circumstances of modern life the principles which guided the garden makers of the Renaissance."

The garden world must have heeded this, because today we are able to visit some of these beautiful Tuscan gardens, many of which are still in private hands but open to the public. In some cases their owners, both Italian and foreign, have spent decades restoring them to their former glory. The Villa Gamberaia is a sublime example, having risen from the ashes of World War II, during which it was burned to the ground. Strolling through its grounds, appreciating the effort and thought that is reflected in its warmth and charm, reminds us yet again how wonderful life can be.

If you want to find out more, see the Suggested Reading section, where I've listed some of my favorite books on Italian gardens. I urge you to slowly stroll through the romantic gardens listed below and allow your senses to savor their beauty and majesty.

RIGHT: An old olive tree laden with fruit sits in a parterre filled with bright pink impatiens.
NEXT PAGE: The Roseto Botanico di Cavriglia's invitation to experience some of the fragrant roses blooming in spring on thousands of lush rose bushes.

"COME INTO MY GARDEN.
I WOULD LIKE MY ROSES
TO SEE YOU"

RICHARD BRINSLEY SHERIDAN

I think one of life's greatest pleasures is watching things grow. That's why I love visiting gardens—especially in Italy. It's a country filled with an abundance of interesting, enchanting gardens, more than one hundred of which are in Tuscany. Explore any garden you come across, for as many curious travelers (or gardeners) know, there are always good ideas waiting to be discovered. Be sure to take time to stop and smell the roses! Although I've never met a garden that I didn't like, the following is a short, diverse list of ones that I revisit again and again, and recommend to all my friends. Before you go here are some tips:

• *All gardens listed here are open to the public except where noted.*

• *You must make an appointment in advance to see private gardens, and a small fee is sometimes required.*

• *Always call ahead or check the websites listed for the most current information on opening times, because in Italy schedules change frequently.*

• *Most gardens are an extension of the magnificent villas they surround. Many of these villas are filled with remarkable works of art and antique treasures and are open to the public—an added dividend!*

• *The book* Historic Houses and Gardens Open to the Public *lists over 1,200 historic stately homes and gardens in Italy and includes their locations, descriptions, schedules (always double check anyway), and even maps. It is published by Editoriale Giorgio Mondadori and is a wonderful companion. It's now available in English as well as Italian (see Suggested Reading).*

• *Remember to wear comfortable shoes, leave your heavy tote bag in the hotel, and bring a pad and pencil for jotting down gardening ideas. Keep in mind that during the summer the midday heat can be scorching, so plan your visit for the morning or afternoon. (Actually, the gardens will probably be closed several hours for lunch anyway, so get in the Italian mode and have a leisurely lunch, too).*

～ ～ ～ ～ ～ ～

Badia a Coltibuono

53013 Gaiole in Chianti (Siena)
011-39-0577-744-81
www.coltibuono.com

Most people visit this out-of-the-way spot, made famous by Lorenza d'Medici, to take cooking lessons (see Chapter Three),

sample good wines and olive oils, or eat a delicious meal. Don't overlook the Renaissance garden tucked in the back, because it is well worth a visit. It is an intimate place with a wonderful feeling of peace, perhaps because Badia a Coltibuono is an old Benedictine abbey that has dispensed hospitality to one and all for over a thousand years. The bounty from their pretty kitchen garden is used in the cooking school and restaurant. The Roseto Botanico (see page 69) is nearby, so you can visit both and have time for a memorable lunch, too.

Boboli Gardens

Piazza Pitti, 1
50125 Florence
011-39-055-218-741

The Boboli is really more a formal park in a small city, with all the characteristics of a large Renaissance garden—in fact, it is the largest of the Medici gardens. Enter through the majestic courtyard of the Pitti Palace, now one of the world's top museums. The first thing I always do is walk up Michelangelo's ramparts, built in 1529, to the Garden of the Cavaliere, one of my favorite spots in all of Florence. Here sits a charming, pale pink building originally used by Cardinal Leopoldo de'Medici as a center for scholars. It's now home to the precious Porcelain Museum surrounded by a panorama of enchanting hills, seemingly unchanged since the sixteenth century. If you're there in May, the lush roses and peonies in the parterre garden will be in full bloom.

Villa Chigi Cetinale

53098 Sovicille
011-39-0577-311-147
By appointment only

Although it's not open to the public, you can call Lord Lambton, the dedicated owner of this magnificent seventeenth-century creation, to view the garden. The predominate feature of Cetinale, located eight miles from Siena, is the long grass allèe that stretches on a main axis east and west of the villa. It guides you from one elegant end to the other through a magnificent brick gateway. This garden has everything: geometric parterres of romantic flowerbeds, beautiful worn brick walls, garden statuary, a hilltop romitorio built in 1716, a lemon garden, and an impressive amphitheater—there's even a lovely old kitchen garden that recently has been restored.

La Foce

61, Strada della Vittoria
53042 Chianciano Terme
011-39-0578-691-01
www.lafoce.com
Open one day a week, or by appointment
After reading *War in Val d'Orcia*, the best-selling diary of Iris Origo written in 1944, I decided I had to see her garden. It is located in southern Tuscany, a region filled with hilltop Renaissance towns that are often overlooked but well worth visiting, such as Pienza, Montalcino, San Quirico, Chiusi, and Monticchiello (see Chapter Seven). After purchasing the estate in 1923, newlyweds Antonio and Iris Origo commissioned English architect Cecil Pinsent to design this now world-famous dramatic and romantic Italian Renaissance creation. There are tours of the garden once per week, and in Chapter One I discussed the possibility of renting one of the beautifully restored farmhouses on the estate. Climbing roses, lemon trees, scented rosemary, thyme, lavender, and luscious peonies all make for a simply gorgeous garden.

Villa Gamberaia

Via del Rosellino, 72
50135 Settignano
011-39-055-697-205
www.villagamberaia.com
Visit graceful Gamberaia, in the small town of Settignano, on a fine morning or afternoon so you can enjoy the breathtaking views of the churches and palazzos of Florence below. Perched on the side of a hill among the olive groves and untouched countryside, this is a quintessential Tuscan garden. It is small and intimate enough to explore at your leisure, and its size makes it easy to relate to, which is why I'm drawn to it. From its parterres of boxwood and ponds, to its intriguing grotto peopled with evocative busts and statues, Gamberaia has been celebrated by discerning guests such as Bernhard Berenson, Edith Wharton, and Harold Acton, who called it "a most poetical garden, a jewel." The Zalum family, who is responsible for the garden's restoration, continues to maintain it to the highest standards, and there are also nicely decorated guest apartments for rent in the old stables.

Giardino Garzoni

Via di Castello
51014 Collodi
011-39-0572-429-131
This famous garden is located in Collodi in the hills surrounding Lucca, the village where Carlo Collodi began writing his classic tale, *Pinocchio*. Its grand seventeenth-century Baroque layout, spread down a hillside, incorporates three imposing terraces, double staircases, overblown flowerbeds, pools, cascades, fountains, and promenades—all linked in a complex theatrical design that has been admired for three centuries. The garden has had its ups and downs, but whatever the case, the eighteenth-century bath house is unique and makes it well worth a visit.

Palazzo Piccolomini

Piazza Pio II
53026 Pienza
011-39-0578-748-503
Seeing this garden is a double pleasure—it's set in the courtyard of the Palazzo Piccolomini, one of the many architectural treasures of the small hilltop town of Pienza, and it's a tiny garden, a true *giardino secreto* (secret garden) enclosed on three sides by a loggia. On the remaining side is an archway through which you can enjoy the stunning views of the Val d'Orcia and majestic Mount Amiata. It has remained unaltered since the fifteenth century and includes the original wellhead and stone garden furniture.

Villa Reale di Marlia

Via Villa Reale
55014 Marlia
011-39-0583-301-08
This grand garden located close to Lucca has a long and distinguished history. Its most famous owner was Napoleon Bonaparte's sister, Elisa Baciocchi, princess of Lucca. She enlarged the estate to regal proportions with the assistance of the designer Jean-Marie Morel, who had been recommended by Empress Josephine because of his work at Malmaison. It is a beautiful garden and includes a large pool with a spectacular fountain, dramatic garden statuary, topiaries, a grotto, and a seventeenth-century *teatro di verdura*, an amphitheater of evergreens where Nicolo Paganini often performed and where concerts are still held today. Its famous lemon garden was the inspiration for a John Singer Sargent painting at the turn of the century.

ABOVE: New life for a huge pottery *orci* jar originally used to store olives.

Roseto Botanico di Cavriglia Carla Fineschi

52022 Cavriglia
011-39-055-966-638
www.rosetofineschi.org
Open only from mid-May through mid-June each year
If you love roses you will be delighted by this very personal garden. In the 1930s, Professor Gianfranco Fineschi's father planted a small collection of antique roses. In the past forty years this orthopedic surgeon's passion has resulted in the Roseto that we see today—over eight thousand individual plants comprising six thousand varieties of roses. When we were there, the colors and fragrances were overwhelming! Due to the vagaries of spring weather, check their website for the ideal days to visit, to see the roses blooming at their best.

Villa Torrigiani

Via del Gomberaio, 3/5
55010 Camigliano
011-39-0583-928-008
This impressive garden has many things to recommend it: remnants of a baroque design by Frenchman André Le Notre, a famous sunken, secret "Garden of Flora," and the *giochi d'acqua*—hidden water jets concealed in stairs, parterres, statuary, and paths, controlled by a gardener who surprised and delighted unwary visitors in the seventeenth and eighteenth centuries. Most of the grounds reflect a later style of English landscape design. If you have time, visit the nearby Villa Mansi and its gardens.

ø ø ø ø ø ø

WORTH NOTING

If you want to spend a hassle-free day visiting some really special Tuscan gardens and villas, just call the well-connected gals at Città Nascosta, a company that specializes in personalized itineraries, who will create a day for you that you will always remember. They have entrée into many exclusive, insider places, and will be delighted to take care of the details (car, guide, etc.) for you and share their love and knowledge of Tuscany.

They also coordinate an event called Toscana Exclusive, which takes place on two consecutive Sundays in May. It's an opportunity to see some of the loveliest historic gardens in the city of Florence and the surrounding countryside—hidden treasures not normally open to the public.
Città Nascosta
Lungarno Benvenuto Cellini, 25
50125 Florence
011-39-055-680-2590
www.cittanascosta.com
info@cittanascosta.it

The Tuscan garden show, Giardini in Fiera, is one of the top horticultural events in Italy, held on the grounds of an ancient Corsini villa in the hills twenty minutes outside Florence. This prestigious fair, over a decade old, showcases the best of the Italian plants and bulbs, garden books, outdoor furniture, and tools, and the most chic garden apparel you can imagine. Created by Olivia di Collobiano and Duccio Corsini, this is where you want to be in mid-September for wonderful garden lectures with international gardening enthusiasts.
Giardini in Fiera, Villa Le Corti
Via San Pietro di Sotto, 1
San Casciano in Val di Pesa
011-39-055-829-301
www.principecorsini.com
info@principecorsini.com

THREE

Taste of Tuscany

The Richness of the Region

"The Tuscans have the faculty of making much of common things and converting small occasions into great pleasures."

—Henry James

Anyone who has ever stood behind an Italian matron buying three tomatoes at a vegetable stall knows how true that statement is. Her discussion with the vendor ranges from what degree of ripeness is necessary (are the tomatoes for tonight or tomorrow?) to how her granddaughter's graduation went, and then back to the tomatoes again, of course.

Tuscany is a region of finely tuned palates. In restaurants it's not uncommon to overhear seemingly endless discussions on the serious business of what to order—is the asparagus fresh, are the mushrooms local, what's the fresh pasta of the day? The always-accurate Marcella Hazan said in *The Classic Italian Cookbook*, "Not everyone in Italy may know how to cook, but nearly everyone knows how to eat." This focus on quality and freshness is why most of us think the food tastes better in Italy than anyplace else on earth. Shopping and eating in step with the seasons is the Italian credo. Is it better to live to eat, or to eat to live? The Italians will always choose the former.

I find it interesting that we who settle for a sandwich or a bowl of cereal at home at the end of a hectic day instantly become gourmets when traveling in Italy, planning where to eat

OPENING PICTURE: A glass of Prosecco wine is a prelude to dining at l'Andana in the Maremma.
OVERLEAF LEFT: Simple ingredients are the staff of life in Tuscany including left, freshly baked bread and right, ripe tomatoes.
LEFT: Local produce on display in Pienza and right, choosing the perfect greens in Florence's Piazza Santo Spirito market.

dinner well in advance and then, once there, dwelling on the menu as if it were our last meal. Are we, too, "converting small occasions into great pleasures?"

Among the many books that my father left me was the Time-Life series *Food of the World*, which I especially treasure. The volume *Cooking in Italy* by Waverley Root contains the best definition of Tuscan food I've ever read: "Tuscany [is] the region where the cooking is thought to be the least 'corrupted' by outside influences. Indeed, the one characteristic shared by the best of Tuscan dishes is a single-minded avoidance of unnecessary complications. Great attention is paid to materials of the highest quality, cooked with a minimum of sauces and seasonings. It is spare home cooking, healthy with no pretense to sophistication. Perhaps that is the highest sophistication of all."

Caterina de'Medici, who married Henry II in 1533, was responsible for bringing the aristocratic elegance of Florentine Renaissance cooking to France (and is said to have introduced the fork to the sophisticated French); at the time the essence of Tuscan food was, as it still is, simplicity. The quality of ingredients is paramount. Much of what one eats and drinks in Tuscan homes and restaurants and buys in the stores is grown nearby. Obviously this means eating according to the seasons—what is freshest at the moment. You won't be eating strawberries in December in too many places in Tuscany.

Italy, especially Tuscany, has been at the forefront of the effort by European countries to pass new legislation promoting sound environmental practices and laws favoring small producers and farmers. It has become the leader in Europe of organic farming. In towns across the region people flock to artisan farmers' markets, like the one in Florence's Piazza Santo Spirito. Called La Fierucola di Pane, it is held on the third Sunday of every month and features everything from whole-grain breads, cheeses, and wines to soap—all one-hundred-percent organic and made in the small farms around the city. (See Chapters Six and Seven for listings of the weekly food markets in each of our favorite towns and cities, including Florence.)

Tuscany is known for its bounteous food markets. In the center of Florence lies the famous Mercato Centrale di San Lorenzo, a tiny city-within-the-city of small vendors where Florentines buy much of their foodstuffs. The glass-domed, two-story cast-iron building provides the perfect place to shop for an amazing assortment of fresh fruits, vegetables, fish, meat, and specialty food items like cheese, olives, pastas, and bread. It is open every day from Monday through Saturday from 7 AM to 2 PM.

RIGHT: In early morning at Florence's two big food markets, you'll find luscious produce like this.
NEXT PAGE: Tuscan favorites include, clockwise, zucchini flowers, artichokes, fennel, and fresh herbs.

BIZERBA

PRODOTTO e VARIETÀ
ZUCCHE
PREZZO
€ 2,00
ORIGINE
ITALIA
CATEGORIA
KG.

There is a smaller market in Florence, the Mercato di Sant' Ambrogio, on the Piazza Ghiberti, ten minutes from the Duomo. Many people feel it is much more authentic, and it is a favorite with the neighborhood locals and fussy food shoppers, who go there for its selection of organic homegrown produce. One booth not to miss is La Botteghina del Augusta dal 1988—it has the most beautiful pasta you've ever seen. The market is open Monday through Saturday from 5 AM to 2 PM.

A concerted effort also is underway by Tuscans who treasure the region's agrarian heritage to keep historic breeds of farm animals from becoming extinct. The Antinori family has been actively involved from the start. Their large vineyard and estate Tenuta Guado al Tasso, in the midst of reclaimed Maremma marshland, now includes a nature preserve with roe deer, wild boar, and pheasants. On the farm estate, we observed the large black-and-white Cinta Senese pigs, distinguished by the thick white stripe that looks like a belt (*cinta*) around their middle. By the 1980s they had almost disappeared, but today they flourish at the farm along with handsome goats and graceful Livorno and Bresse chickens. The Antinoris started with forty pigs and are now up to two-hundred thirty, and their fifty chickens have multiplied to seven hundred. The flavorful products from these animals are delicious and much sought-after.

In the 1980s a wonderful movement called Slow Food was started by energetic Italian journalist Carlo Petrini. The idea behind the organization was to protest the spread of fast-food spawned by globalization and instead return to consuming the locally grown, natural foods eaten in the past. It's the Slow Food belief that, this way you are eating something fresh and healthy, while at the same time supporting local farmers and artisinal food producers. Sound thinking! Petrini has said: "Our defense should begin at the table with Slow Food. Let us rediscover the flavors and savors of regional cooking." If you'd like to join the worthwhile organization, see page 218.

Slow Food products and the stores that sell them bear the sign of a small snail, which is the organization's logo. This movement has grown tremendously, with branches in about fifty countries including the United States, and it is taken quite seriously in Tuscany.

In 1992 another step in the direction of healthier food was the European Union's designation of two prestigious categories to protect quality agricultural and food products derived from their own geographical environment: DOP (denominazione di origine protetta) and IGP (indicazione geografica

ABOVE: During the harvest, plastic rakes are used to release ripe olives from the trees without bruising them or pulling off many leaves. They will then be taken for processing and made into the flavorful extra virgin olive oil for which the region is known.

RIGHT: There is nothing like bringing a loaf of fragrant, freshly baked Tuscan bread to the table.

protetta). You will see the special blue-and-yellow European Union seal on Tuscany's many fine food products in the food stores and weekly markets throughout the region (see Chapter Seven).

Tuscan cuisine is dominated by bread and olive oil—which is one of the many reasons that we love this area. Bread has always been a staple of the diet: fourteenth-century miniatures dedicated to Boccaccio's *Decameron* feature the distinctively shaped *pane toscano*—the typical bread of this region. The loaf is oval, the crust is crunchy, and the texture has irregular pockets of air, similar to sourdough. When we were at Tenuta Guado al Tasso, the

highlight of the weekend was the baking of this traditional bread as a treat for the children. It was made in a 130-year-old oven using two-year-old starter called *madre del pane*. The fresh, warm bread tasted better than gelato!

Tuscan bread is unique because it is made without salt (*sciocco*). One reason for this is because there were onerous salt taxes levied on Florentine bakers in the twelfth century. Another is that the thrifty townspeople decided it would be wasteful to add anything more to their bread since their food was already so rich and flavorful. Because the bread lacks salt, it absorbs moisture very slowly and can last several days before becoming hard—though

Marcella Hazan's advice is "it is not insulting to bread to call it stale, because freshness is merely the first of its many lives." Tuscans have taken things a step further. Whether toasted, rubbed with garlic, and drizzled with extra virgin olive oil (*fettunta*), spread with chicken liver paste to make *crostini*, floating in a bowl of thick rustic soup (*ribollita*), or crumbled into a summer salad, after two thousand years Tuscan bread still tempts us.

Aldous Huxley once said, "If I could paint and had the necessary time, I should devote myself for a few years to making pictures only of olive trees." My husband and I have been told that there are about seven million olive trees in Tuscany (who counted them, we always wonder?). As you drive through the countryside—from the gentle hills of Siena to the wild coast of the Maremma and the peaks of Pisa—everywhere you look you see the gorgeous, silvery-branched trees for which this region has been known since Etruscan times.

In late fall, usually November, the harvest begins and the olives are ready to be handpicked and pressed. Some are peppery and intense, some sweet and fruity. The fresher the olive oil, the better the taste, the more intense its bite. The range of flavors is vast and each olive oil tastes differently.

On my most recent trip to Tuscany, my husband and I visited with noted food expert and author Faith Willinger in her big Florentine kitchen where she gives cooking lessons. It was wonderful finally to meet someone whose articles I had been clipping from food magazines for years. "First rate extra virgin olive oil is the reason that food tastes so wonderful in Tuscany," she explained. I had never thought about this before. It's so simple, but so true: olive oil is healthy and delicious, and Italian cooking as we know it would not exist without it. It is a main ingredient in Tuscan cooking—not just an accent.

Local demand for top olive oils is so great that as a result only a small percentage is available for export. Many of the region's top wine producers, such as the Antinoris and the Frescobaldis, make their own extra virgin oil from olives grown high in the Chianti hills—for example Laudemio, a prize-winning blend of several different olive varieties made to the highest standards. In addition there are many, many small producers making top-quality oils such as Castello di Capezzana, Castello di Volpaia, Tenuta di Cafaggio, and one of Willinger's favorites, Castello di Ama. (If you want to order the real thing to sample at home, see Chapter Eight).

During our October travels along the coast, we spied olives being harvested earlier than usual on a hilltop that faced the warm ocean breezes. Cloths called *racanà* were spread under

LEFT: Drive through the lush Tuscan countryside in late fall and you will see this scene on almost every hillside. The olive harvest begins with cloths spread under the trees to catch every last one. The *terroir*, or climate, altitude, and soil, in which the olives are grown, will determine the quality of the oil that will be made from them just as it does for wine.

LEFT: A lovely alfresco lunch at La Vigne, a restaurant just outside Radda in Chianti country.
ABOVE: Cinzia Ninci bakes *pane toscano*, saltless Tuscan bread in a one hundred-year-old oven at Guado al Tasso.

the trees to catch the olives that fell when the branches were shaken with hand-held rakes. We started taking photographs and as we finished and prepared to leave, the owners of the *fattoria* rushed out of their house carrying a plate of warm *fettunta* and a bottle of red wine. Then their elderly father emerged from the nearby stone mill (*frantoio*) with a pitcher of just-pressed bright green olive oil, which they drizzled over the warm bread—it was heavenly and unexpected, an exceptional Tuscan moment for us.

A recent newspaper food column stated, "Good news, nothing new in Italy." It noted with incredulity that you can still get the most astonishingly good, classic food in Italy, and this is especially true in Tuscany. Even with globalization and fusion cuisine making its way into some trendy Florentine eateries, tradition prevails. Most restaurants still adhere to the age-old precepts of *la cucina povera*, economical home cooking, using the bounty of the local produce rather than expensive imports to create their simple but always flavorful dishes.

SCEGLI I FORMAGGI

CUGUSI

	€ KG	
PECORINO FRESCO		10,10
PECORINO MEDIA STAGIONATURA		11,50
PECORINO ROSSO TRATTATO CON CONSERVA DI POMODORO		12,00
PECORINO AL TARTUFO		19,00
PECORINO AL PEPE		13,00
PECORINO AL PEPERONCINO		13,00
PECORINO STAGIONATO		14,00
PECORINO STAGIONATO SOTTO CENERE		14,50
PECORINO GRAN RISERVA		17,00
PECORINO STAGIONATO SOTTO FOGLIE DI NOCE		17,00
RICOTTA		4,91
RAVIGGIOLO (LA CONFEZIONE)		1,80

 PRODUZIONE PROPRIA

Reassuringly, Tuscan cuisine has remained true to itself.

Crostini, pork *salumi*, and sausages still start off most meals. Hearty rustic soups follow, many made with beans and day-old bread. Pastas are topped with tomato sauces and meat ragùs. Roasted meats and fowl predominate as the main course; pork roast is ever popular, and steaks called *bistecca alla Fiorentina* are king. Vegetables are eaten raw or simply cooked and cheese tops the dessert list, along with almond-flavored *cantucci* (biscotti) that is often served with a glass of Vin Santo, a sweet dessert wine—always a perfect ending to a delicious meal (if you still have room)!

One of the wonderful benefits of working on this book was that we sampled some of the most delectable food imaginable. Whether at an internationally renowned restaurant in Florence or a tiny *trattoria* in the country, each meal was a joy (see Chapters Six and Seven for some of our favorites).

It wasn't only what we ate. Everywhere we went, people wanted to share their love of food, wine, and of Tuscany. Some places were simple in the extreme—almost extensions of the small kitchen in the back. Many restaurants use "Buca" in their title; literally "buca" means hole, and often describes a restaurant or trattoria located below street level. Two of our

PREVIOUS PAGES: There are many kinds of Pecorino cheeses made in Tuscany: *Pecorino nero* (black) and *Pecorino rosso* (red) shown at right.
RIGHT: The Tuscan countryside offers a bit of everything from fragrant lavender and sweet cherries to spicy peppers and pungent cheeses.

perennial favorites, Buca dell'Orafo in Florence and Buca di San Francesco in Arezzo, are anything but.

One of our favorite stops is a trattoria called Casa Mia in the tiny village of Montefiridolfi close to the beautiful *agriturismo* Fonte de'Medici. Everyone warned us to make a reservation (011-39-055-443-92) because the place is very small, but they didn't say how small. When we arrived, all of the six tables were taken, except the one they had saved for us (with a wink)—"the one with a view." It faced out through the front doorway, which was hung with a multicolored beaded curtain about three feet from the seldom-used main road in town. The friendly owner suggested the specials of the day, including homemade pasta and sweet early peas in season with butter, and we were on our way to experiencing one of those exceptional Tuscan moments. What was remarkable about the meal, aside from the great food, was that with each course, we set out new silverware for ourselves from the drawer in the table we were eating on. Do-it-yourself, Tuscan style.

So that you too can eat like a Tuscan, we've listed the regional specialties that you are sure to encounter on a typical Tuscan menu. There are many variations on a theme—for example, *cacciucco di Livorno*, the classic fish stew, is made with different fish and ingredients depending on which part of the Tuscan coast you are on. And, although grated Parmigiano-Reggiano cheese is served with almost all pasta dishes, it originates in the Emilia-Romagna region, so it's not highlighted.

There are many different types of eating establishments in Italy, and as life becomes more casual the exact lines that define them become blurred. A *ristorante* is a restaurant, usually sophisticated, with a professional kitchen and wait staff, and a complete menu. A *trattoria/osteria* is usually family-run, serving unpretentious local food in simple surroundings; the *pizzeria*, originating in the south of Italy in the Naples area, is now ubiquitous and popular throughout the region. An *enoteca* is a wine store, sometimes with a wine bar offering snacks and light local specialties. A *bar* is usually a place to stop for a quick espresso, alcoholic or non-alcoholic drink, small sandwiches (*panini* or *tramezzini*) or pastry (we always order at the bar as the Italians do—to eat at a table can cost twice as much); a *caffè*, historically a coffeehouse, is now synonymous with bar, often with tables both inside and outside for having a morning *cornetto* (croissant) and cappuccino or lingering over an afternoon drink with friends. A *pasticceria* is a pastry shop, and a *gelateria* is where you can buy delicious homemade ice cream and pastries.

LEFT: Tuscan restaurants are called by many different names including *cantina, pizzicheria,* and *trattoria*. "*Cucina casalinga*" or homemade food, means you are probably in for a really pleasing treat.

It is important to note that in Italy there is a certain formality and order in which the courses are served. Two courses are never brought to the table at the same time. Each has its reason for being and is a prelude to the next. Whether it's breakfast (*colazione*), lunch (*pranzo*), or dinner (*cena*), one thing you can be sure of—you will eat well. *Buon appetito!*

HOW TO EAT LIKE A TUSCAN
Antipasti

Typically every meal starts with an antipasto. These appetizers are classics with rustic overtones that get you started on the ritual of the anticipated meal ahead. When dining in someone's home, you usually are offered an antipasto with an aperitif before you are seated at the table, and then a second one when you sit down. *Crostini* and *salumi* top the list.

Crostini—*Crostini* are round, toasted pieces of crusty bread topped with a variety of meat or vegetable pates, and are featured in almost every antipasto spread in Tuscany. The following are some examples:

• *Crostini di Fegatini*—Beloved by all, the traditional topping of chopped chicken liver pate.

• *Crostini alla Toscana*—An assortment of toppings includes arugula with olive oil, olives, and capers.

• *Crostini Bianchi*—A San Gimignano favorite made of butter, cheese, and truffles.

Here are some variations on the crostini theme:

• *Fettunta*—A large slab of toasted bread rubbed

RIGHT: The mouth-watering *fettunta* we were offered by a friendly local family.

with garlic and salt and drizzled with a generous amount of extra virgin olive oil. Ever popular but most enjoyable in late fall, when the oil is harvested and at its freshest.

• *Bruschetta*—*Fettunta* topped with fresh chopped tomatoes and basil.

• *Panzanella*—A summer favorite of cold chopped tomatoes, basil, and olive oil and pieces of stale bread softened with water and vinegar.

• *Antipasto alla Toscana*—A plate of regional Tuscan cured meats—*salumi*, sausages, and *prosciutti*—served with toasted bread on the side.

Salumi—Tuscany is world-famous for its pigs and the various pork products derived from them. A fine art, *salumi*—known in the United States as salami and sausages—are found in many varieties, shapes, and sizes. The following are the most common:

• *Finocchiona*—The most famous, this large salame is flavored with fennel seeds and spices. Soft and coarse-grained, it often falls apart when sliced and is sometimes called *sbriciolona*, which means crumbly.

• *Salame Cinghiale*—Made from ground wild boar meat, it is air-cured and leaner than many of the other salumi.

• *Soppressata*—A large pressed salame made with various spices and lemon peel.

• *Salame Toscana*—A large salame studded with peppercorns.

• *Lardo*—Thin slices of pig fatback seasoned with aromatic herbs and cured in a salt brine.

• *Prosciutto di Toscana*—A Tuscan ham that is cured for nine months and has a robust taste. It is darker and stronger than those of the Parma region.

Primi Piatti

In Italian primi piatti means "first plates," and this first course almost always takes the form of a pasta or soup. These days many Italians who are eating lighter will order only a primo piatto after their antipasto and then move on to dessert.

Soups—Traditional soups in Tuscany are very important, and hearty servings featuring beans or vegetables, often thickened with day-old peasant bread, are popular. (Tuscans are often called *i mangiafagioli*, or "the bean eaters," by other Italians.)

• *Ribollita*—Reboiled or twice-cooked soup defines this thick bean mixture, made with seasonal vegetables and served over pieces of bread.

• *Pappa al Pomodoro*—A smooth, thick mixture of tomatoes, bread pieces, garlic, and basil.

• *Acquacotta*—Literally "cooked water," this hearty soup contains vegetables, a beaten egg, and thick bread.

• *Zuppa di Fagioli*—This simple vegetable soup is dominated by cooked cannelli beans with bread.

RIGHT: A plate of flavorful Tuscan cured meats, which you will see almost everywhere in the region includes, clockwise top, *salame toscana, lardo, finnocchiona, prosciutto* and, center, *filetto di maiale*.

- *Zuppa di Funghi*—Thick mushroom soup to be looked forward to in the fall, when many Tuscans go wild mushroom hunting.
- *Zuppa alla Frantoiana*—A Tuscan classic made with bread and peppery black winter cabbage.
- *Zuppa di Farro*—Made with the Tuscan grain farro, vegetables, and *pancetta*.
- *Stracciatella*—Chicken broth, beaten eggs, and parmesan, seasoned with salt, pepper, and nutmeg.

Pastas—This is the quintessential Italian food, always served in small portions and with a variety of sauces. Most popular in Tuscany are simple tomato-based sauces such as *pomarola*, made with the bounty of fresh summer tomatoes, or ragùs, chopped meat sauces made with boar, duck, hare, or veal. Seasonal treats include vegetable sauces made with mushrooms, artichokes, truffles, and pumpkin, and the like. The names of the individual types of pasta vary from region to region in Italy, but the ones you are most likely to find in Tuscany are:

- *Pici* or *Pinci*—A thick, fat version of spaghetti.
- *Tagliatelle*—Handmade ribbon-shaped strips of pasta about a quarter of an inch wide.
- *Pappardelle*—Like *tagliatelle*, only three quarters of an inch wide.
- *Ravioli*—Squares of pasta typically filled with ricotta cheese, spinach, or butter and sage.
- *Tortellini*—A type of *ravioli* in the shape of a half moon.

LEFT: Pasta comes in all shapes and sizes from hand-made *pici* to more robust cheese and vegetable ravioli and even delicious spinach *gnocchi* the size of golf balls.

GIUGGIOLE
1€/ht

Secondi Piatti

The main, and often the most important, course in any Tuscan meal, the secondi piatti generally comprises meat, fowl, game, or fish served with fresh local vegetables.

- *Bistecca alla Fiorentina*—A two-inch thick T-bone steak from cattle of the Val di Chiana region of Tuscany, known for its tasty, juicy beef. It is seared over hot charcoal, seasoned only with salt, pepper, and olive oil, and usually served rare *(crudo)*. This dish is ordered by weight in a restaurant.
- *Arista di Maiale*—Named from the Greek *"aristos"* meaning "the best," this Tuscan favorite is a succulent pork loin with garlic and rosemary and other herbs.
- *Stracotto*—A pot roast cooked slowly tender with tomatoes and red wine until very tender.
- *Scottiglia*—A stew of various meats and poultry cooked with tomatoes.
- *Pollo alla Diavola* or *Al Mattone*—A "mashed" chicken that has been pressed flat with a brick and cooked with hot spices and herbs over a hot wood fire.
- *Cacciucco alla Livornese*—A classic fish stew originating on the Livorno seacoast, it can include many kinds of fish such as squid, octopus, scallops, or cod.
- *Trippa alla Fiorentina*—A Florentine favorite, small pieces of tripe cooked with tomato sauce and vegetables and then baked with a covering of parmesan cheese.

Contorni

The literal translation of contorni means "contours," meaning to fill out the plate, give the meal shape, and add colors and flavors. Seasonal vegetables such as fennel, eggplant, baby onions, mushrooms, squash, asparagus, and artichokes are stuffed *(ripiene)*, sautéed, grilled, braised, or eaten raw.

- *Pinzimonio*—A platter of the freshest raw vegetables served with a small dish of extra virgin olive oil seasoned with salt and pepper.
- *Fagioli all'Uccelletto*—White beans cooked with tomatoes, sage, and olive oil. They are also cooked in a straw-covered wine bottle and called *fagioli al fiasco*, or simply cooked in oil for *fagioli all'olio*.
- *Fiori di Zucca Fritti*—Vegetables battered and deep-fried are a Tuscan favorite. This includes zucchini flowers, artichokes, squash and carrot slices, black kale *(cavolo nero)*, and cardoons *(cardi)*, a vegetable similar to celery.
- *Insalata Verde*—After the *secondi piatti*, many Italians have a small green salad of fresh daily produce such as arugula, chicory, mesculun, and a wide variety of lettuce greens.

Formaggi

Italians rarely eat sweet desserts, preferring instead to end the meal with a macedonia, or fresh fruit cup, or a plate of figs or cheese, often paired with a nice red Tuscan wine.

LEFT: Contorni or vegetables are very important in the Tuscan diet and include everything from *pinzimonio* to olives, squash, peppers, and my favorite, zucchini flowers.

Pecorino is the cheese of Tuscany; it is made from sheep's milk and has been enjoyed since Etruscan times. It is often still called *cacio* locally, which is the ancient term for cheese.

The most famous *pecorino* cheeses made from ewe milk are produced south of Siena near Pienza and Montalcino, where the sheep graze on the verdant green hills. You'll find several types in Tuscan food stores and restaurants. *Pecorino marzolino*, made in early spring (traditionally, March), is a mild soft cheese when fresh. It becomes semi-hard and tangy when aged for six months and is called *stagionato* at this stage. You'll see stacks of small wheels of it piled up in food stores, some coated with ash and called *Pecorino nero*, or coated with tomato paste and called *Pecorino rosso*. *Pecorino romano*, made in Grossetto, is aged and hardened for grating.

Dolci

When Tuscans want something sweeter for dessert it is usually a type of biscotti or *cantucci* (hard cookies) or cake based on dried fruit or nuts. In Florence the exceptions are a Florentine cheese tart and *zuccotto*, a dome-shaped cake inspired by the Duomo made of liquor-soaked pound cake, chocolate, chopped nuts, and whipped cream.

• *Cantucci*—Twice-baked hard cookies, usually served with Vin Santo for dipping.

• *Buccellato*—A small cake in the shape of a ring, filled with candied fruits.

• *Pan Forte di Siena*—A flat cake of candied fruit and spices sweetened with honey.

• *Ricciarelli*—Marzipan almond-flavored cookies.

• *Castagnaccio*—A flat cake of chestnut flour paste, pine nuts, and candied fruit.

Caffè

A meal in Italy is never complete without a strong cup of *caffè* (espresso) to finish it. This tiny amount of intense liquid should be sipped alone after dessert. Of course, Italians also enjoy espresso several times during the course of the day as a pick-me-up. Italians consider cappuccino to be a breakfast drink, a substantial way to start the day, and so it is never, ever ordered after lunch or dinner. And don't expect a lemon peel with your espresso—that is an American affectation.

Variations on the espresso theme include: *caffè doppio*, a double shot; *caffè macchiato*, with a dollop of foamed milk; *caffè decafinato* (decaffeinated); *caffè corretto*, with a splash of grappa or brandy; and *caffè lungo/Americano*, espresso diluted with hot water and sometimes served in a large cup. *Latte macchiato* is milk with the addition of espresso. If you order just a latte (à la Starbucks), you will end up with a glass of milk!

RIGHT: Make a bottle of the Italian cordial Limoncello at home. Place the peel of 6 lemons and 3 cups of vodka in a large jar. Let stand for 2 weeks. Then boil 3 cups of water and 1 cup of sugar until dissolved. Allow to cool and add to the vodka mixture. Let stand for a week. Then chill and enjoy.

While we are on the subject of good things to drink, let's discuss one of the most important aspects of Tuscan life, wine—or as Hugh Johnson, author of *Tuscany and Its Wines*, calls it, "the landscape in a bottle." Like bread or olive oil, it is a daily part of life. It would be almost unthinkable to have a meal without it. Even in the most humble trattoria, one of the first conversations with the waiter will be about what wine to order: a carafe of the reasonable, local house wine (*vino della casa*), usually young and easy to drink, or something more serious and expensive, for example, a fine bottle of Tignanello. It's a complicated subject, with such a long history and so many variables that wine expert Johnson noted that "a sense of humor is almost as important as a corkscrew in the confusing world of Italian wine."

Today, a great many of the best wines in the world come from Tuscany, but it wasn't always so. From the 1930s to 1950s, Tuscan wines were produced in small vineyards with little concern for real quality, except among a handful of growers whose wines were not usually exported. In 1963, the Italian government attempted to bring order to the industry and created a system to standardize the country's wines, bringing them up to international standards of quality. This legislation established a minimum criteria for each wine before it could be awarded a rating of either DOC or DOCG, a system still firmly in place today.

To be rated DOC (Denominazione di Origine Controllata), a wine has to meet many criteria, including using only certain approved grapes and a percentage of each, be grown in a specific zone, adhere to color, flavor, and alcohol content standards, and be aged for a minimum period of time. DOCG (Denominazione di Origine Controllata e Garantita), requirements are even more rigorous.

Tuscany has been *the* center of Italian wine for hundreds of years, but the significant growth in production and worldwide recognition of its high quality has come about in the past thirty years. Many date the real revolution in fine Tuscan wines to the early 1970s, when Marchese Piero Antinori of the noble Florentine family took over the reins of his company, which had a wine making history dating back to 1180. By combining progressive methods with traditional ones, bypassing the limitations of the existing Italian classifications, he along with some of the other wine-making families redefined Italian wine to what it is today. A new appellation called IGT (Indicazione Geografica Tipica) was created to classify these wines.

The first of these wines, now known as "super-Tuscans," was Sassicaia, created by Antinori's uncle Mario Incisa della Rocchetta and the great wine maker Giacomo Tachis, and

LEFT: The wine harvest occurs in the autumn when luscious grapes like these are ready to be harvested. NEXT PAGE, LEFT: Wines stored in wood vats in the cellars at Badia al Coltibuono and right, wine that was able to be bottled in the isolated monastery in the mid-1940s during World War II.

marketed under the Antinori label. It was a great success. In 1970 the Antinoris created another, Tignanello, and the trend continues to this day.

Today super-Tuscans are among the most highly esteemed wines in Italy. It is said that they are responsible for strengthening the reputation of all red wines in Tuscany. We visited the Antinoris' wine estates in Chianti and the Maremma regions where the super-Tuscans were born. They have built a new winery on their Guado al Tasso property, located near the town of Bolgheri in the Maremma, which since the mid-1990s has been the wine frontier in Tuscany. The Antinoris' partnership with Napa Valley's Atlas Peak created a wine that was a leader of the Cal-Ital trend, produced in California from grapes traditionally associated with Italy. Antinori has said, "I love wine because it never comes to an end. It is always in a state of evolution, and I always feel I can make it better. It keeps me close to nature."

The Frescobaldis are another great family of wine producers in Tuscany, and one of the oldest, with more than a seven-hundred-year tradition in the arts and culture in Italy, especially in Tuscany. They have been producing outstanding wines for thirty generations; and in fact in the sixteenth century they were supplying wine to many European countries and to the royal family of England as well. They have files documenting sales to King Henry VIII. They presently have nine estates, including Castello di Nipozzano, Castello di Pomino, Castel Giocando, Tenuta Castiglioni, and Tenuta Santa Maria, each of which produces wines appropriate to their different soils. In 1995 they teamed up with California producer Robert Mondavi in a joint venture at Castel Giocando in Montalcino.

While the Antinoris and Frescobaldis may be the largest wine producers, in Tuscany there are 160,000 acres of vineyards owned by over 4,000 vintners. Names that are familiar to anyone who enjoys good wines include Badia a Coltibuono, Castello di Brolio, Castello di Fonterutoli, Castello Banfi, Barone Ricasoli, Ruffino, and Biondi Santi. The thread that ties most of them together is the Sangiovese grape, which results in wines ranging from light, easy to drink Chiantis to powerful Brunellos. And let's not overlook the Avignonesi family, who makes the exquisite dessert wine Vin Santo.

Here is a selection of some important wines in Tuscany:

• *Chianti*—A word that is synonymous with Tuscan wines, for many years, "Chianti" conjured up an image of a 1960s Italian restaurant filled with tables covered in red-and-white checked tablecloths, topped with straw-covered *(fiasco)* wine bottles used as candlesticks. This was due to the long period of Chianti overproduction that

RIGHT: The Marchese Piero Antinori and his three daughters, left to right, Allegra, Albiera, and Alessia of the Antinori wine dynasty and some views of grapes growing in their vineyards.

occurred in Tuscany in the 1950s and 1960s, when growers focused on quantity instead of quality, and the reputation of Italian wines suffered as a result. Fortunately, all of that has changed.

• *Chianti Classico*—This is produced in the zone that lies in the heart of the area between Florence and Siena. Any wine from this area that meets specific standards of the Gallo Nero Consortium proudly wears the Gallo Nero (Black Rooster) label on the neck of its bottle. The term *riserva*, controlled by Italian wine laws, is only used for wines that have extra aging. Chiantis that have been aged for three years either in wood or in the bottle can be labeled *riserva* if they qualify as a wine of premium quality. Riservas are not produced every year, as the grapes must be the choicest and come from a good harvest of an especially good year.

• *Brunello di Montalcino*—Often called the superior wine of Tuscany, it is produced by more than a hundred vineyards and estates. Large, wide-mouthed goblets have been specially designed for drinking Brunello so as to expose this rich, full wine to more oxygen. It is always in demand because its production is limited and it needs ten to fifteen years of aging. It is made in the hills around the charming town of Montalcino (see Chapter Seven).

• *Vino Nobile di Montepulciano*—Once called the "king of all wines" by the poet Francesco Redi, it was the preferred wine of the noblemen in the seventeenth century—hence its name. It is aged a minimum of two years in wood barrels and is only made from the Sangiovese grape in the region of Montepulciano (see Chapter Seven).

• *Vernaccia di San Gimignano*—White wines have never been dominant in Tuscany, with the exception of Vernaccia. Considered Tuscany's best white wine, it is made from ancient vines (Michelangelo mentioned it in his writings) in the vicinity of San Gimignano near Siena (see Chapter Seven).

• *Vin Santo*—"Holy wine" is the literal meaning of this sweet wine pressed from Malvasia and Trebbiano grapes that have been hung up to dry for a period of several months so the sugars are concentrated. It is then aged in small wooden barrels for at least three years. Traditionally served with dessert, such as simple cakes and fruit tarts, this golden wine often accompanies the especially hard dipping cookies called *cantucci*.

These wines, the essence of Tuscany, are a gift from a fruitful land and have been prized since ancient times. They embody the word "*terroir*," or, literally, the taste of the earth. This poetic statement by John Mortimer, in *Rumpole and the Blind Tasting*, says it all: "The point of drinking wine is to get in touch with one of the major influences of Western civilization, to taste the sunlight trapped in a bottle, to remember some stony slope in Tuscany. . .'

FAR LEFT: Wine is everywhere you look in Tuscany.
NEAR LEFT: The chic Frescobaldi Wine Bar in Florence.

On one of our many adventures in Florence we met the delightful Benedetta Vitali who was co-founder of the popular Florentine restaurant Cibreo. She now owns Zibibbo Trattoria, a restaurant tucked away in a corner of the city and one of the hottest spots in town. It's the perfect place to have a leisurely lunch or dinner, away from the hustle and bustle, overlooking the surrounding treetops.

Benedetta cooks some of the most delicious food—both traditional and creative. An energetic person who generously shares her love of cooking, she invited us to attend one of her cooking classes. We have included the recipes for the dishes we cooked, so you can make an authentic Tuscan meal at home.

Chicken Liver Crostini

Scoop and serve as a pâté or spread on toasted bread.

1 cup extra virgin olive oil
1 red onion, finely chopped
1 carrot, finely chopped
1 celery stalk, finely chopped
1 pound chicken livers
1 smashed garlic clove
2 tablespoons capers
1/2 cup milk
1/4 cup cognac
1/2 stick softened butter
1 loaf of crusty Italian bread

Heat the oil over medium heat in a large skillet. Add the chopped vegetables, stirring continuously until golden.

Add the chicken livers, garlic, and capers and sauté for 30 seconds. Then add the milk and Cognac. Cook for 10 minutes.

Puree mixture in a food processor until creamy and immediately stir in the butter.

Refrigerate for several hours. Serve with slices of toasted bread.

Serves 6 people.

RIGHT: A plate of chicken liver crostini and far right, delicate Pomarola sauce served on pasta.

Pomarola Sauce

The secret to this sauce's rich taste is the butter added before serving.

1/2 cup extra virgin olive oil
3 garlic cloves, coarsely chopped
2 pounds fresh diced tomatoes or
   a 28-ounce can of San Marzano tomatoes
15 fresh basil leaves
salt and pepper to taste
2 tablespoons unsalted butter
1 pound spaghetti
1 cup freshly grated parmigiano-reggiano cheese

Bring 4 quarts of salted water to a boil, so that you can start cooking the pasta when the sauce is almost done.

In a saucepan heat the olive oil for 1 minute. Add the garlic and cook until soft, about 1 to 2 minutes.

Add the tomatoes, basil, salt, and pepper. Simmer uncovered for 20 minutes, stirring occasionally.

Cook the pasta according to the directions until al dente and drain.

Add the butter to the hot sauce, stir immediately into the pasta, and serve with freshly grated parmigiano-reggiano cheese.

Serves 6 people.

Fried Zucchini Flowers

Benedetta says you can also try this recipe with artichoke hearts.

18 zucchini flowers
2 cups all-purpose flour
1/4 teaspoon salt
1/4 cup white wine
water
2 cups extra virgin olive oil

To wash the flowers, fill a bowl with water. Carefully dip each blossom and gently dry it by hand on a paper towel.

Combine the flour and the salt in a mixing bowl, slowly whisking in the wine until smooth. Gradually add water 1 tablespoon at a time until the batter is liquid. Dip your finger in the batter, and if it is covered by a light film, it is ready.

Chill for 1 hour.

Heat the oil in a large skillet for 2 minutes until very hot but not smoking.

Using tongs, dip each zucchini flower in the batter, place it in the oil and cook, turning once until golden brown.

Drain on paper towels, sprinkle with salt, and serve hot.

Serves 6 people.

RIGHT: Fried zucchini flowers start the meal and, below, a Florentine cheese tart completes it.

Florentine Cheese Tart

This light dessert is a Zibibbo favorite.

For the crust:
2 cups cake flour
1/2 cup sugar
1 egg yolk
1 stick softened butter
1 tablespoon water

For the filling:
8 ounces cream cheese, at room temperature
8 ounces Marscapone cheese
1/3 cup sugar
6 tablespoons orange marmalade
1/2 cup sliced almonds

Preheat oven to 400 degrees.

To make the crust, put all the ingredients in a large bowl and knead into a ball. Let rest for 4 hours.

Use a 9"-diameter tart pan with a removable bottom and coat with nonstick spray. Press the dough evenly over the bottom of the pan and up the sides.

Bake at 400 degrees for 15 minutes. Let cool.

Remove the crust and slide onto a platter.

For the filling, combine the cheeses and sugar in a large bowl and beat with a spoon until creamy.

Fill the crust with this mixture and refrigerate for 2 hours.

Before serving, cover with marmalade and garnish with sliced almonds.

Serves 6 to 8 people.

If you love to travel, cook, and eat, an ideal trip should include cooking classes. Given that Tuscan cuisine is so popular, it's no surprise that around almost every corner there's a cooking school or someone giving lessons. To get you started we thought we'd list our recommendations—from chefs who give private lessons, to formal cooking schools. All classes are taught in English.

In Florence our favorites are Benedetta Vitali of Zibibbo Trattoria; Faith Heller Willinger, the noted food expert and author; Giuliano and Sharon Oddson Gargani of Trattoria Garga; and Giuliano Bugialli, with whom we took cooking lessons many years ago in New York City and who is now teaching in Tuscany.

Market to Table Cooking Classes

Faith Heller Willinger
011-39-055-233-7014
www.faithwillinger.com

Faith calls herself a born-again Italian (her words)—and she really is. She moved to Italy from the United States in 1973 and was seduced by Italian regional cooking, and since has spent more than thirty years searching for the best food and wine from the Alps to Sicily, with no regrets about mileage or calories (her words too)! She lives in Florence with her Tuscan husband and is the author of *Eating in Italy* and the ever-popular classic *Red, White and Greens*.

She teaches Market-to-Table cooking classes to a maximum of six participants in her Florentine kitchen. Each class starts with a morning visit to the nearby Santo Spirito market on Wednesdays, which is when her favorite farmers are there. After that it's back to the kitchen for an espresso and extra virgin olive oil tasting. Then it's time to cook the meal, from antipasto to dessert. This is followed by a lunch of what you have cooked, paired with her favorite important wines. When class is over you'll go home with a goodie bag.

She and her assistant, Jennifer Schwartz, also do a personalized half-day Food Lover's Tour of Florence. They specialize in keeping up with the latest food trends and happenings, and the walking tour includes tastings, sipping, and hunting for culinary souvenirs in the places that they've discovered. For anyone who loves food, this is a great way to see Florence. At the end of this chapter is a tempting list of places Faith recommends.

Zibibbo Trattoria Cooking School

Benedetta Vitali
Via di Terzollina, 3/r (Florence)
011-39-055-433-383
www.zibibboonline.com

Benedetta Vitali offers two cooking course options in her beautiful trattoria. She gives an intensive Monday-through-Friday class covering the fundamentals of cooking that is limited to two participants. The mornings are spent in hands-on sessions learning to prepare important dishes such as *soffritto*, the classic vegetable foundation of many Italian dishes; various meat, fish, and vegetable stocks; six simple sauces and pastas; techniques for frying vegetables and meats; and how to make some of Zibibbo's popular mouth-watering desserts. Lunchtime is spent discussing the day's subject and analyzing wines.

In addition, Benedetta offers a monthly Saturdays in the Kitchen class, which is held on four consecutive Saturday mornings for a maximum of eight people. Be sure to sign up in advance, because this is a way for many Florentines to spend a weekend morning.

La Cucina del Garga

Giuliano and Sharon Oddson Gargani
Via delle Belle Donne, 3 (Florence)
011-39-055-211-396
www.garga.it

The dynamic owners of the trend-setting restaurant Trattoria Garga offer several options to those who want to learn how to cook with brio. Canadian-born Sharon Oddson Gargani has twenty years of experience working in the internationally known restaurant that she owns with her ex-husband and has started a cooking school that features two options. One Day in Florence starts in the morning with a trip to the market to buy the necessary provisions and then continues from noon to four in the restaurant's kitchen where the small class cooks an Italian meal.

Four- or eight-day programs are held in southern Tuscany. You'll live in a hotel and cook in Sharon's farmhouse. Highlights are forays to nearby vineyards and sheep farms to sample the local pecorino, and even a visit to beautiful La Foce. Part of each day is spent in hands-on preparation of the meal.

ABOVE: Benedetta Vitale (left) teaches a Saturday morning cooking course in her restaurant.

Cooking in Florence

Giuliano Bugialli
252 Seventh Avenue #7R
New York, NY 10001
646-638-1099
www.bugialli.com

Giuliano Bugialli, the famous Italian chef, television personality, and cookbook author, teaches a one-week, fully hands-on cooking class just outside of Florence. The classes are offered three times per year. Participants stay in a hotel in the center of Florence, and a shuttle bus takes the entire class on the short ride to and from the new kitchens. Space is limited to sixteen to twenty people.

Two cooking schools in Florence take a more formal approach to cooking: Apicius, the Culinary Institute of Florence, and Scuola di Arte Culinaria Cordon Bleu. Both award various types of degrees and require a considerable time commitment, as most of their courses run for at least a semester.

Apicius, the Culinary Institute of Florence

Via Guelfa, 85 (Florence)
011-39-055-265-8135
www.apicius.it

The Culinary Institute of Florence is located in the city center and is directed by Gabriella Ganugi. Offering a broad academic and professional program, its curriculum is designed for those interested in preparing for professional careers in the culinary arts, hospitality management, wine, food communication and design, and marketing for the food industry. In addition, there are weekly courses on food and wine and customized programs that anyone can sign up for.

Scuola di Arte Culinaria Cordon Bleu

Via di Mezzo, 55/r (Florence)
011-39-055-234-5468
www.cordonbleu-it.com

This school was established in 1985. The founders, Gabriella Mari and Cristina Blasi, are members of the Cordon Bleu de France and focus on the regional cuisine of Italy and basic Italian cooking. If you are just visiting, you can sign up for a Taste of Tuscany, a two-hour hands-on lesson devoted to cooking a three-course Italian meal.

Badia a Coltibuono

53013 Gaiole in Chiani (Siena)
011-39-0577-744-832
www.coltibuono.com

There's a wonderful cooking school and vineyard in the upper woodlands of the Chianti region, just south of Siena, that is world-famous. Located in an ancient monastery built by Benedictine monks in the eleventh century, Badia a Coltibuono, which means the "abbey of good harvest," is the perfect place to indulge your love of food, wine, and cooking.

The Stucchi-Prinetti family has owned Badia a Coltibuono since 1846. It became known worldwide over twenty years ago, when Piero Stucchi-Prinetti opened up the gates to visitors and his wife Lorenza de'Medici began her famous cooking school and started writing her beautiful, best-selling cookbooks.

Their four children, Emanuela, Paolo, Roberto, and Guido, now head up various divisions of the business, and their vitality permeates every nook and cranny of this wonderful place. There's something happening all the time. There are tours of the Renaissance villa and enchanting garden (see Chapter Two). The vast vineyards have become one of the most successful winemaking operations in Italy, and their olive oil is enjoyed the world over, so there are tours of the old wine cellars followed by wine and olive oil tastings.

Badia a Coltibuono is known for its outstanding cooking courses. The five-day residential program means staying in this splendid, fresco-walled Renaissance villa and experiencing the joys of the Tuscan countryside. Taught by chef Francesco Torre and other visiting food experts, students learn how to prepare a meal from bread to dessert and enjoy it afterwards in the villa's elegant dining room. Also featured are a combination of Tuscan gastronomic and cultural activities. Private cooking lessons can be arranged.

If you don't have time for the course or the tours, you can still visit the magnificent abbey and have lunch in the wonderful restaurant on the property, savoring the delicious fresh cooking and the outstanding wines.

～ ～ ～ ～ ～ ～

Nowadays many hotels offer cooking lessons featuring well-known chefs and include trips to local, artisinal food makers. What better way to learn about Tuscany than to be able to cook your way through the region?

Villa San Michele School of Cooking

Via Doccia, 4
Fiesole (outside Florence)
011-39-055-567-8200
www.villasanmichele.com

The Villa San Michele is an idyllic place to stay if you're looking for a peaceful vacation. This luxurious hotel is located in the Fiesole hills above Florence with one of the best views of the city. Signing up for cooking lessons is a perfect way to relax and have a once-in-a-lifetime experience. Classes are held in the Villa's kitchen in the morning or afternoon and are taught by famous chefs such as Giuliano Hazan, Anton Mosimann, and

ABOVE: Paolo, Emanuela, and Guido Stucchi-Prinetti sample a glass of wine at Badia a Coltibuono.
RIGHT: Chef Francesco Torre working in the kitchen.

Raymond Blanc. The large selection of programs range from two to four sessions and are open to ten participants. There is also a Tuscan Wine Week featuring daily wine tastings, children's cooking lessons, and a wide choice of pasta classes.

Relais and Restaurant Il Falconiere

Localita San Martino, 370
Cortona (Arezzo)
011-39-0575-612-679
www.ilfalconiere.com

Il Falconiere is located near Cortona in the picturesque countryside where Tuscany meets Umbria. The owners Silvia and Riccardo Baracchi are the hosts at this charming Relais and Châteaux property. Their cooking program, Cooking Under the Tuscan Sun, is a hands-on six-day course limited to fourteen people. Cooking lessons are held by the chef and staff of the hotel, and tours of the area cover the beautiful nearby towns of Cortona, Pienza, and Montalcino. There are also expeditions to the Baracchis' favorite artisanal food and crafts producers and many memorable meals and wine tastings.

Food Lover's Tour of Florence

The following are some of Faith Willinger's favorite places to shop and eat in Florence. If you want to know more about her Food Lovers Tour of Florence, see page 118 in this chapter.

FOOD SHOP
Baroni Alimentari
Via Galluzzo
011-39-055-289-576
www.baronialimentari.it
Located at the Mercato Centrale, they have great cheese, wine, salumi, and Faith's favorite Castello di Ama extra virgin olive oil, which they will ship home for you.

SIMPLE LUNCH
Nerbone
Mercato Centrale di San Lorenzo
011-39-055-219-949
Have a traditional boiled beef sandwich at this classic.

FAVORITE CAFFÉ
Caffè Ricchi
Piazza Santo Spirito
011-39-055-215-684
Wonderful sketches of the nearby Church of Santo Spirito hang on the walls in this caffé.

WINE BARS
Fuori Porta
Via Monte alle Croci, 10/r
011-39-055-234-2483
www.fuoriporta.it
Choose from a huge wine selection and observe the young Florentine crowd.

Pitti Gola e Cantina
Piazza Pitti, 16
011-39-055-212-704
Enjoy the great location, with tables outside in the piazza.

GELATO
Carabè
Via Ricasoli, 60
011-39-055-289-476
Their yummy ice cream includes special flavors like pistachio, hazelnut, and almond—and it's terrific in summer for the best granita ices outside of Sicily.

NEW BAKERY
Dolcissimo
Via Maggio, 61
011-39-055-239-6268
www.caffeitaliano.it
The elegant pastries, beautiful cakes, and just-baked *cornetti* in the mornings all come in pretty packaging.

FOUR

The Artisans

Tuscan Creativity and Style

"Oh, what I would give for an Italian sense of style."

—Barbara Grizzuti Harrison

In Italy there has always been a connection between the country's beauty and exquisite artistic riches and its inhabitants' good taste and style. It's a sensibility reflected in day-to-day life, often down to the smallest detail, and is the very reason why for many of us being in Italy is so irresistible. There is pride in small things well done—one flawless peach carefully wrapped in a brown paper bag, a white shirt ironed to pristine perfection. What other nation could take a simple after-dinner walk, the *passeggiata*, and turn it into a national pastime—a lovely occasion to stroll arm-in-arm down sophisticated city streets, meeting and greeting friends, and checking out the latest fashion trends in the always chic shop windows.

This sensibility is manifested everywhere: in the design of a sublimely embroidered jacket or a pair of impeccably crafted shoes; the gracefulness of a hand-carved gilt Baroque frame; the smooth lines of a sleek Ferrari or yacht; the fecundity and wit of home design—from furniture, lamps, tableware, ceramics, and silver down to everyday household basics such as a can opener or lemon juicer. In Italy, attention is always paid to quality and to detail.

Since the Renaissance, Tuscany—and especially Florence—has been home to artisans of every persuasion, and the tradition of craftsmanship is still strong in a region that still

makes things. As you walk the city you will notice old street names like Via degli Arrazzieri, "street of the tapestry makers," or Via della Spadai, "street of the sword makers." A dedication to the old-world tradition of artisanal crafts passed down through the generations (apprenticeship in the workshop of an established master craftsman is still common) and to making things by hand with skill and pride is still alive and well.

In her 1959 book *The Stones of Florence*, Mary McCarthy describes Florentines as being extremely gifted in mending and fixing old things to make them last. This is still true. Wandering the back streets between the Pitti Palace and the Church of the Carmine, you pass workshops that repair everything from wobbly dining room chairs to treasured family heirlooms. Whether you are interested in mosaics, painted furniture, or anything in-between, you'll find someone here on the Oltrarno who can craft it, repair it, or restore it, and I've included a select list by category at the end of this chapter. As a longtime antiques collector, the fact that one can get almost any object beautifully repaired here has always delighted me. A walk on the other side of the Arno uncovers some of the most wonderful artisan studios and workrooms you'll ever see.

To begin, one of the most famous

OPENING PICTURE: A work in progress at Pietra di Luna, Florence, using *scagliola*, an ancient art in which pigments and powders are used to create colorful tabletops and panels.
OVERLEAF LEFT: Laudomia Pucci near a Pucci-clad mannequin on an opulent settee at the Palazzo Pucci and right, ceramic hens on display at a Tuscan ceramics fair.
RIGHT: A colorful leaded glass window at Locchi, where beautiful crystal objects are made.

generational woodcraft families in the world is located here—Bartolozzi e Maioli. Founded just before World War II they restored the bombed monastery in Monte Cassino and recently rebuilt a nineteenth-century section of the Kremlin. Gaia Bartolozzi and her mother now run the evocative shop on the Via Maggio crammed with magnificent hand-carved objects, everything from chandeliers and sconces to tables and chairs.

We always stop to say hello in two other special places—the ateliers of silversmith Paolo Pagliai and glass artisans Locchi, where Florentines have been buying beautiful objects for as long as anyone can remember. Paola Locchi and her daughter-in-law Giovanna head an atelier that has been restoring, grinding, and carving crystal since work was first commissioned by the Grand Duke of Tuscany in the nineteenth century. And for years the Pagliai family has been repairing, engraving, and embossing silver from around the world, including treasures from the Vatican in Rome.

Next, take a trip back in time at Antico Setificio Fiorentino, a textile workshop in the San Frediano section of the Oltrarno. They have been supplying sumptuous silk damasks, taffetas, and brocades to the Florentine aristocracy since the Renaissance. It has been in its current location since 1786, but its archives date back to 1492. In the 1950s, Emilio Pucci, Florentine designer and a descendent of one of Florence's founding families, came to its rescue when it was about to go under. His family still owns and runs it today.

Exquisite fabrics are woven by ten master

weavers who learned their craft from their parents and grandparents before them. Ancient looms are still used, including a unique wood-warping machine called an *orditoio* based on a design by Leonardo da Vinci. On a visit to their workshop you'll see lavish fabrics, including silk taffetas woven in three antique weights, in more luscious colors than you can imagine, as well as authentic rustic Tuscan linens. The best part is that you can actually buy something from their scrumptious selection of pillows, frames, and other fabric items. Or you can make an appointment with longtime director Sabine Pretsch to look through the intriguing old pattern books and order something custom-made for your home.

Another fascinating stop is a visit to Lorenzo Villoresi, who is the hottest perfumer in town, with a client list of the rich and famous from around the world. He custom blends exceptional fragrances in an atelier at the top of his elegant medieval house with a breathtaking view of Florence, creating magic out of the thousands of essential oils that fill the bottles on floor-to-ceiling shelves and perfume the air. He will create a scent especially for you, or you can choose from one of the delicious fragrances available.

No discussion about Tuscan workmanship would be complete without touching upon ceramics and terracotta. If you prefer terracotta (unglazed ceramic), then you should make your way out of Florence to the nearby town of Impruneta where stacks of huge, gorgeous garden pots and ornaments are piled up outside the many shops.

The town of Montelupo Fiorentino is well known for its glazed ceramics—sophisticated reinterpretations of classical Renaissance patterns updated for modern lifestyles. There is a ceramics museum here, with pottery going back to ancient times. The streets of the town are lined with ceramics stores and workshops like Flavia, owned by the Bitossi family, featuring the dynamic pieces of Aldo Londi. Outside of town is Dolfi, a ceramics factory that makes the stunning, oversize ceramic pieces you often see in fashionable stores like New York's Bergdorf Goodman. There is also a school in the town that will teach you everything you ever want to know about making ceramics.

If you enjoy learning vacations and have always wanted to learn how to paint, what could be nicer than spending a week taking lessons on a verdant hillside in southern Tuscany? The art of plein air, open-air landscape painting, had its origins in Italy in the seventeenth century, with visiting French artists initiating a classical tradition of painting outdoors that lasted almost two hundred years. Maddine Insalaco and Joe Vinson of Etruscan Places have diverse backgrounds in drawing, painting, and art history and have lived in Italy for years. They

LEFT, CLOCKWISE: Jewel tones of paper taffeta at Antico Setificio Fiorentino; intricately carved wood objects at Bartolozzi e Maioli; precious perfumes at Lorenzo Villoresi; and typical rustic Tuscan pottery.

ABOVE: Sketches from their vast archives serve as a backdrop for an ornate silver candelabra at elegant Pampaloni, one of the oldest silver shops in Florence where those in the know go for tabletop treasures.

have used their expertise to put together a wonderful program that will get you painting Italian style. They take care of all the details, including catering delicious alfresco lunches of local specialties in the midst of the farms, vineyards, and olive groves where you'll be painting (see page 133 for details).

Fashion is another art where Italians traditionally have excelled. During the Middle Ages, Florence was the center of the fashion industry, importing wool from England and France and weaving it at immense profit. Shoemakers and goldsmiths reportedly were given the same status as artists and sculptors. Even in this age of consumerism, it's impossible not to be overwhelmed by the exquisite luxury in Italian shops—clothing, shoes, handbags, jewelry—all sophisticated, well-designed, and impeccably made.

In the early 1950s Italy reemerged as an important force on the international fashion scene and started its successful climb to the top.

Gucci, Pucci, and Ferragamo, three trend-setting Florentine companies, started to make their mark in a big way, and they are still going strong today. I attended some of the glorious fashion shows held those early days in the opulent White Room of the Pitti Palace and it was magical. The most memorable were those of Emilio Pucci, whose sleek dress and accessory designs in vibrant, bright colors exploded within the white, austere walls of the ballroom.

Avid skier Marchese Emilio Pucci, a member of Italy's Olympic team, founded his fashion house in 1947 because his aristocratic friends couldn't find chic ski clothes. For decades his company led the avant-garde fashion pack with its wonderfully timeless, colorfully printed silk jersey clothing and accessories. Florentines have always adapted to change and now Marchesa Cristina Pucci, Emilio's wife, and their daughter Laudomia are re-energizing one of the hottest fashion successes ever. Their extensive fashion archives in the Palazzo Pucci, in the heart of Florence where the family has lived since the fourteenth century, are a source of inspiration to the company and also the core of the Pucci Foundation, whose elegant research center will be open to fashion historians, journalists, and students once completed.

In *Sprezzatura*, a wonderful little book, authors Peter D'Epiro and Mary Pinkowish say that "functionality and beauty are the very essence of Italian civilization." The definition of *sprezzatura*, the Renaissance code of conduct, is

ABOVE: Plein air painting in the cultivated hills near San Gimignano.
NEXT PAGE: Artisan David Matassini working in his shop Neltempo in Radda.

that every action should be carried out with effortless grace. That something be done with panache and an air of nonchalance is still an important part of Italian life. The notion of *la bella figura* (to cut a fine figure, or make a good showing), an Italian preoccupation noted by Machiavelli in the fifteenth century, is also very much in play. As is the case in so much of the world today, in Italy beauty is not deemed superfluous. It is important. Here, life and art merge totally—innately.

Events

Fiera della Ceramica
Arte della Ceramica
Associazone di Ceramisti
Via Campicuccioli, 26b
Localita Paterno, Palago
011-39-055-830-1075
Every year at the beginning of October a spectacular show of terracotta pottery and ceramics is held in Florence in the Piazza S.S. Annunziata. Over fifty talented artisans from Tuscany and other parts of Europe come together to display their wares, which range from traditional ceramic techniques to the most modern designs. Prices are usually reasonable.

Fierucoline
Associazone di Ceramisti
Via Campicuccioli, 26b
Localita Paterno, Palago
011-39-055-830-1075
Fierucoline means "small fairs," and they take place in towns all over Tuscany. Our favorite occurs in Florence in the Piazza Santo Spirito on the third Sunday of every month except for August and features craftspeople like soap makers, basket weavers, wood-carvers, and knitters just to name a few. Look for Alesandro Bruni who carves the most beautiful dishes and salad servers from olive wood, burnished to a high sheen with olive oil.

International Ceramics Festival
Ufficio Turistico
Via Baccio da Montelupo, 43
Montelupo Fiorentino
011-39-057-518-993
www.comune.montelupo-fiorentino.fi.it
For one week each June there is an international ceramics festival in the town center of Montelupo Fiorentino, just about 15 miles from Florence. The streets are lined with exhibits, outdoor workshops and demonstrations, and a ceramic market offering a wide selection of wares.

∽ ∽ ∽ ∽ ∽ ∽

Museums

Museo Montelupo
Pottery and Archeological Museum
Via Bartolomeo Sinibaldi, 45
50056 Montelupo Fiorentino
011-39-0571-513-352

For those who love ceramics, this is a wonderful museum with an impressive collection of documented pottery from the earliest prehistoric times to the nineteenth century, with special emphasis on majolica. If you are interested, an extensive restoration laboratory is open to visitors by appointment.

∽ ∽ ∽ ∽ ∽ ∽

Schools

CERAMICS
La Scuola di Ceramica
Via Caverni, 163
50056 Montelupo Fiorentino
011-39-0571-541-111

LANDSCAPE PAINTING
Etruscan Places
10 Ashland Street
Newburyport, MA 01950
212-780-3216
011-39-0577-806-351
www.landscapepainting.com

MOSAICS
Opificio delle Pietre Dure
Via degli Alfani, 78r
Florence
011-39-055-265-111

∽ ∽ ∽ ∽ ∽ ∽

Artisans

ALABASTER
Cooperativa Artieri
Piazza dei Priori, 5
56048 Volterra
011-39-055-0588-875-90

Paolo Sabatini
Via Matteotti, 56a
56048 Volterra
011-39-058-881-515

CERAMICS
Bartoloni
Via Garibaldi, 36
50056 Montelupo Fiorentino
011-39-0571-512-42

Ceramica ND Dolfi
Via Tosco Romagnola Nord, 8/b
50056 Montelupo Fiorentino
011-39-0571-910-105
www.otellodolfi.it

Flavio
Via A. Gramsci, 16
50056 Montelupo Fiorentina
011-39-0571-514-03

Studio d'Arte Fratelli Taccini
Via Provinciale di Mercatale, 252
50059 Vinci
011-39-0571-508-081

Ceramiche Rampini
Casa Beretone di Vistarenni
53017 Radda in Chianti
011-39-0577-738-043
www.rampiniceramics.com

Neltempo
Silvia and David Matassini
Viale G. Matteotti, 1
53017 Radda in Chianti
011-39-0577-738-158

CRYSTAL
Locchi
Via Burchiello, 10r
50124 Florence
011-39-055-229-8371
www.locchi.com

CUSTOM-MADE SHOES
Mannina
Via Barbadori, 23r
Florence
011-39-055-282-895

Roberto Ugolini
Via Michelozzi, 17r
Florence
011-39-055-216-246

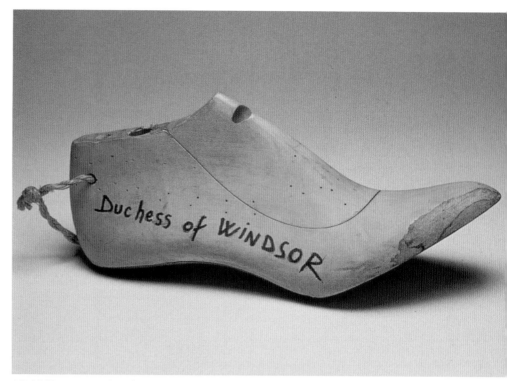

ABOVE: A wooden last at Ferragamo who has custom made the shoes of many famous celebrities including the Duchess of Windsor.

Stefano Bemer
Borgo San Frediano, 143r
Florence
011-39-055-211-356

FASHION
Emilio Pucci Boutique
Via dei Tornabuoni, 20r
50123 Florence
011-39-055-265-8082

Salvatore Ferragamo
Via dei Tornabuoni, 2
50123 Florence
011-39-055-336-0456

FRAMES
Cornici Artistico Santo Spirito
Piazza Santo Spirito, 17r
Florence
011-39-055-239-8139

Leone
Via del Porcellana, 61r
Florence
011-39-055-282-090

GOLD LEAF
Francheschi Severino
Via Lorenzo Bartolini, 7r
Florence
011-39-055-289-992

HANDMADE PAPER
Giulio Giannini e Figlio
Piazza Pitti, 36r
Florence
011-39-055-212-621

LAMPS
Il Paralume
Borgo San Frediano, 77–79/r
Florence
011-39-055-239-6760
www.ilparalume.it

LEATHER

Scuola del Cuoio
Piazza Santa Croce, 16
or
Via San Giuseppe, 5r
50122 Florence
011-39-055-244-533
www.leatherschool.com

METALWORK

Ubaldo Baldini Bronze Foundry
Via Palazzuolo, 101r
Florence
011-39-055-210-933

MOSAICS

Arte Decorativa di Simone Fiordelisi
Via dei Barbadori, 41r
Florence
011-39-055-215-766

G. Ugolini
Lungarno degli Acciaiuoli, 66r
Florence
011-39-055-284-969

Pitti Mosaici
Piazza dè Pitti, 23/r
50125 Florence
011-39-055-282-127
www.pittimosaici.it

Raffaello Romanelli
Lungarno Acciaioli, 72/78r
Florence
011-39-055-239-6662
www.arca.net/mall/romanelli

PAINTED FURNITURE

Ivan Bardi
Via del Presto di San Martino, 4r
Florence
011-39-055-287-967

Autentiqua
Via del Presto di San Martino, 20r
50125 Florence
011-39-055-282-935
www.autentiqua.it

PERFUME

Lorenzo Villoresi
Via de' Bardi, 14
Florence
011-39-055-234-1187

Officina Profumo di Santa
Maria Novella
Via della Scala, 16
Florence
011-39-055-230-2437

PORCELAIN

Studio Santo Spirito
Via della Sprone, 19r
Florence
011-39-055-214-873

SCAGLIOLA

Pietra di Luna
Via Maggio, 4r
Florence
011-39-055-265-8257

SILVER

Pampaloni
Borgo S.S. Apostoli, 47r
Florence
011-39-055-289-094

Paolo Pagliai
Borgo San Jacopo, 41r
Florence
011-39-055-282-840

TASSELS

Passamaneria Valmar
Via Porta Rossa, 53r
Florence
011-39-055-284-493
www.valmar-florence.com

TERRACOTTA

Mario Mariani
Via di Cappello, 29
50023 Impruneta
011-39-055-220-1195

Zago Terrecotte
Via Mazzini, 136
50027 Strada in Chianti
011-39-055-858-338

Ugo Poggi
Via Imprunetana, 16
50023 Impruneta
011-39-055-201-1077

TEXTILES

Antico Setificio Fiorentino
Via L. Bartolini, 4r
50124 Florence
011-39-055-213-861
www.setificiofiorentino.it

Busatti
Lungarno Torrigiani, 11/r
50123 Florence
011-39-055-263-8516
www.busattifirenze.com

WOODWORKING

Bartolozzi e Maioli
Via Maggio, 13r
50125 Florence
011-39-055-239-8633
www.bartolozzi.net

Castorina
Via Santo Spirito, 13r
Florence
011-39-055-212-885
www.castorina.net

Daniele Nencioni
Villa Maffia, 54r
Florence
011-39-055-212-195

FIVE

Connoisseurs' World

A Timeless Passion

"Everyone knows the difficulty of things that are exquisite and well done—so to have facility in such things gives rise to the greatest wonder."

—Baldassare Castiglione

In 1528 Baldassare Castiglione wrote *Il Libro del Cortegiano* (The Book of the Courtier). It established the rules for refined behavior and manners based on Renaissance humanist ideals and examined the question of how Italians could live a civilized, artful life. The book was translated into many languages and became a best-seller in Europe until well after the French Revolution. Along with a mind-boggling list of personal accomplishments that included the study of Latin and Greek in addition to other languages, Castiglione wrote that a cultured person should pursue an appreciation of aesthetics in music, poetry, and the visual arts, including painting, sculpture, antiquities, and all manner of beautiful objects.

It was a time when applied crafts were blooming simultaneously with the fine arts and in many cases they were equally ranked, resulting in the rare objects that we call antiques. Goldsmith and sculptor Benvenuto Cellini worked his magic in magnificent decorative objects of gold, silver, enamel, ivory, tortoiseshell, and mother-of-pearl. Potters invented new shapes in majolica, a type of tin-glazed earthenware, and had them decorated by well-known artists. Filippo Brunelleschi was a silversmith as well as an architect, and Luca della Robbia worked in earthenware as well as marble. This powerful tradition of comingling the fine arts with crafts of unmatched quality has made Tuscany a fertile hunting ground today for a vast variety of exquisite antique objects that are avidly sought-after.

In 1852, American art and antiques collector James Jackson Jarves said when he moved to Florence that it was "the world's capital of bric-a-bracdom." He become an art historian, and the rare objets d'art he acquired over the forty years he remained there are now in the United States. His important collection of Tuscan art objects is at Yale University and his Venetian glass is at New York's Metropolitan Museum of Art.

If you too are passionate about antiques, a good place to start is Florence, with its hundreds of antiques shops. They are not places for bargains. Instead, they feature desirable, one-of-a-kind merchandise that you won't see anywhere else. I've listed some good stores in Chapter Six that is all about Florence. If you are there in September, don't miss the Biennale Antiques Show, also listed. Every Tuscan town has its quota of antiques stores, ranging from top notch to "you-never-know-what-you-will-find" junk shops (see Chapter Seven for favorites in each specific town).

Most Italians need go no further than their own family attics to unearth a wealth of valued objects. When acquiring them, they draw upon Italy's exceptional inventory of more than two

OPENING PICTURE: The Pope's Hall at La Suvera with its vaulted ceiling and elaborate fireplace.
OVERLEAF LEFT: A seventeenth-century painting of a church interior sits behind a life-size marble statue of the Marchioness Campana Tenerami, who was a pupil of Canova and right, the statue of a goddess.
RIGHT, ABOVE: An eclectic collection of antique objects and below, a Napoleon-inspired interior.

thousand years of outstanding design patrimony, ranging from Renaissance pieces to twentieth-century Art Deco and Art Moderne, and decorate their homes with enviable ease and flair.

To experience this genius for layering antiques, art, and history up close (and learn more about antiques), there's no better spot than the splendid Relais La Suvera, an Italian country house hotel. It is near Pievescola, a tiny hamlet between Florence and Siena in the gentle unspoiled countryside of southern Tuscany, which you can peacefully explore to your heart's content along the way. Driving through La Suvera's graceful iron gates into the courtyard, you enter another world. The imposing Renaissance villa in front was built in the twelfth century as a fortress. Four hundred years later, it was owned by Pope Julius II. In 1989, along with the surrounding ancient stone buildings and charming chapel, it was transformed into a hotel (details on page 188).

You will be enthralled by the interiors, because the delightful owners Marchese Giuseppe Ricci Paracciani Bergamini, his wife, Principessa Eleanor Massimo, and their daughter Elena are passionate collectors and have decorated La Suvera with rich, centuries-old art and antiques. The Marchese has a wonderful eye for the exceptional and the

FAR LEFT: Elena Ricci Paracciani Bergamini and left, the historic façade of the Papal Villa at La Suvera dating back to the twelfth century, splendidly transformed by the Ricci family.

extraordinary. The tasteful furniture, paintings, sculpture, carpets, silver, ceramics, metalwork, and textiles are astonishing treasures "from a few family palaces," as he puts it. Each antique piece has been harmoniously arranged with exquisite Italian élan, to create a beautiful still life—a rare painting propped up against a mantle piece, Etruscan jars marching up steep stone steps.

Each room has a theme and tells a story, and several are named after the Riccis' aristocratic ancestors. Just imagine staying in the "Room of Angels" with its richly hued floor-to-ceiling eighteenth-century painted tapestries and waking up in a seventeenth-century damask canopy bed. Or you might choose the shimmering green Napoleon Room, with its School of David portrait of the emperor, Imperial furniture, and Aubusson carpet, and a bathroom featuring a collection of thirty-three Capodimonte porcelain statuettes of Napoleon with his troops. Each room has a folio with descriptions of the art and antiques, including their history and provenance, for interesting and educational late-night reading.

I am naturally curious, and loving antiques as I do, I invariably try to peek into some of the other thirty-two rooms and suites of the hotel. Each room is decorated with one-of-a-kind pieces. The opulent reception rooms—the Pope's Hall, the library, the music room, and the Hall of the Marchioness Campana—with their intarsia marble floors and classical architectural details, and with their high vaulted ceilings and loggias,

are cool spots to relax after a day of sightseeing.

What you might expect is a stuffy formality in a place like this, but that isn't the case. The Riccis are dignified, urbane, warm people who love history and antiques and enjoy sharing that interest with others. They are sympathetic hosts who have created a rare refuge filled with beauty, but they haven't forgotten the important details. Even though you may feel like their houseguest, every convenience is at hand—including a competent, friendly staff.

This is a place where you can simply relax. My perfect day is to spend a lazy morning in the spa, then take a swim in the beautiful heated pool. Before you know it, it's time for a light lunch at the Bar dei Limoni, the poolside restaurant. After a short nap on crisply ironed linens, with a good book in hand I settle into a chic wicker chaise overlooking the magical garden and sunlit views of the Sienese hills. Then it's dinner and time to enjoy one of the estate's award-winning wines, finishing off with the best homemade vanilla gelato. A New York friend of mine who loves everything about Italy suggested that we stay at La Suvera and said that we'd love it more than any other place we'd ever been. She was right. From the moment we arrived to the moment we left, all I could think about was when we would return.

After catching the antiques bug at La Suvera, get ready to "shop till you drop" at the biggest outdoor antiques market in Italy: you will need every ounce of energy you can muster. It takes

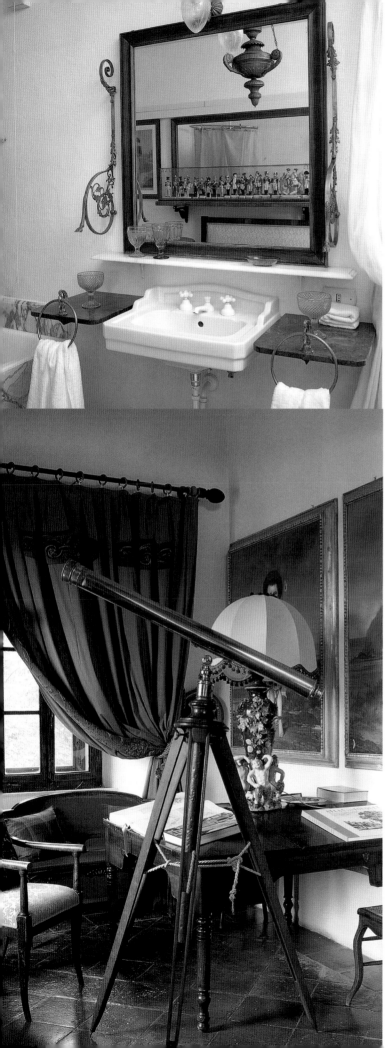

place in Arezzo (only an hour from La Suvera), an important Tuscan city that should be visited. Arezzo was home to many of the great men of the Renaissance and Middle Ages—the poet Petrarch, the satirist Arentino, the architect Giorgio Vasari, and the painter Piero della Francesca, to name a few. It has been featured in many films, including *Life Is Beautiful*. The memorable scene of Roberto Benigni rolling down the red carpet was photographed on the steps of its famous Duomo, and the picturesque Piazza Grande played a supporting role.

One of the oldest towns in Tuscany, Arezzo's history goes back to Etruscan times when it was a center of pottery making and metalworking. Because of its prized hilltop location, surrounded by four different valleys, the city was in endless conflict with Florence, which is reflected in the fortress-like aspects of its crenulated towers. Although the town was heavily bombed during World War II, leading to the rise of its modern outskirts, it has retained its pristine historic center with many outstanding architectural features. The Piazza Grande, the town's largest square, is home to the Palazzo delle Logge, designed in 1573 by Giorgio Vasari, and the Pieve di Santa Maria, a gem of a twelfth-century Romanesque church with ornate carvings.

But Arezzo's true claim to fame is the Church of San Francesco, which contains painter Piero

LEFT, ABOVE: A bathroom at La Suvera with antiques including statues of Napoleon and his troops.
BELOW: A library filled with antique books, many treasures, and a nineteenth-century telescope on a tripod.

della Francesca's greatest masterpiece, *The Legend of the True Cross.* These magnificent frescoes tell the complicated story of the wood used to make the cross of the crucifixion. It took della Francesca fourteen years to paint it, and the frescoes are considered the best examples of Renaissance painting in Tuscany. They are magnificent, having recently been restored to their earlier splendor, and are located in the apse of the church. Our favorite restaurant in town, Buca di San Francesco, is just next door if you want a bite to eat afterwards.

The neo-Gothic cathedral, or Duomo, houses several remarkable stained glass windows by Frenchman Guillaume de Marcillat, who worked in the Vatican with Michelangelo and Raphael before moving to Arezzo. While you are in town, take the opportunity also to visit Petrarch's birthplace, Casa del Petrarca, and the home of Vasari, Casa del Vasari.

If you are an antiques enthusiast and are lucky enough to be visiting Tuscany on the first weekend of the month, you have a real treat in store. That's when the remarkable Arezzo Antiques Fair takes place in the historic town center. Just imagine—five hundred antiques dealers displaying their varied wares along winding streets, narrow alleys, shady courtyards, and even church steps. And this is in addition to the more than one hundred local antiques shops (our favorites are listed on pages 148–149).

Everyone from specialized collectors and connoisseurs to those in search of a good deal will have, as the Italians say, "the pleasure of discovery" perusing Arezzo's antiques (*antichità*) and artworks. You'll find a little bit of everything: Italian, English, and European silver; a wide range of pottery and ceramics; prints and engravings dating back to the seventeenth century; rare and used books; religious artifacts; scientific instruments; watches; and metalwork. Then, there is the furniture: nineteenth-century Empire, thanks to the influence of Napoleon and his court in Italy; lots of Stile Floreale, the Italian Art Nouveau; and 1930s sleek Art Deco. There are also more modern collectibles (*anticaglia*) such as tin toys, musical instruments, vintage clothing, and jewelry, not to mention furniture and home accessories by the now-famous designers that emerged after World War II. The lively scene is punctuated by visitors who flood the streets looking for that certain something. If you have the strength to hang on until Sunday at sunset, when the dealers start to pack up, you might be able to negotiate a real bargain. All you need to know is: *quanto costa questo?* (how much does this cost?) and *mi fa lo sconto?* (will you give me a discount?).

RIGHT, CLOCKWISE: Views of the Arezzo Antiques Fair: painted wood putti sit on a carved chair; a dealer takes a break; a view of the town's square filled with a treasure trove of antiques that spill down into the narrow streets; and George, the fair's friendly mascot, stands guard.

It's a snap to get to Arezzo. You can drive there via the Autostrada A1, but parking is problematic (it's only worth it if you plan on buying big pieces). We always take the train, which is easy and fast. It's a direct shot from the Santa Maria Novella train station in Florence and the trip takes anywhere from a half hour to over an hour, depending on which train you take. Log on to www.raileurope.com (888-382-7245) before you leave so you can earmark the intercity trains that are the quickest. When you arrive in Arezzo and exit the terminal, you can actually see some of the dealers' stalls a mere five-minutes walk away. No reason, or time, to get lost today!

Remember to take some empty tote bags, a small magnifying glass, a cell phone, moist towelettes, and some fruit to keep you going. Wear comfortable shoes, sunscreen, and a jacket with lots of pockets where you can safely keep your valuables. You will need to bring cash or travelers' checks in Euros—very few take credit cards. Don't forget to get a receipt with a description and date of the item. If the object is over a hundred years old, you will not have to pay American duty at customs on your return. And remember to bargain, it's an Italian tradition.

Fiera Antiquaria Arezzo
Arezzo Antique Fair
Throughout the entire town
011-39-0575-377-993
www.arezzofieraantiquaria.it
www.arezzoantiquefair.com
The first Sunday of each month and the Saturday before.
Open all year
8 AM to 8 PM

Antiques Shops

There are loads of terrific antiques shops in Arezzo to explore if you happen to miss the antique fair. Most also are open during the weekend of the big antiques show. Here are a few of my favorites, including two shops that carry beautiful hand-woven bed and table linens, Busatti and Sandro De Santis.

Antichità Giorgio Vaiani Lisi
Corso Italia, 50
011-39-0575-324-634

Antichità Luisa Buroni
Via Cavour, 9
011-39-0575-403-030

Antichità Paolo Burzi
Corso Italia, 22
011-39-0575-302-284

Galleria Antiquaria Giano
Via Cavour, 8
011-39-0575-351-936

Grace Gallery Antichità
Via Cavour, 30
011-39-0575-354-963

La Belle Époque
Piazza San Francesco, 18
011-39-0575-355-495

Tempi Moderni
Piazza Grande, 28
011-39-0575-300-598
www.tempimoderniarezzo.it

HAND-WOVEN LINENS

Busatti
Corso Italia, 48
011-39-0575-355-295
www.busatti.com

Sandro De Santis
Via G. Vasari
011-39-0575-352-769

Restaurants

If you are like me, the last thing you want to do in the midst of a tempting antiques show is stop for a long lunch. In this case, however, you should make an exception. You'll have a special experience at the famous restaurant Buca di San Francesco. Buca means "hole" or "cave," and this restaurant is set into a medieval cellar just next to the famous Church of San Francesco, featuring fourteenth-century frescoes. It is owned by the charming Mario de Filippis, who serves delicious local specialties typical of the area with a dollop of his homegrown philosophy. The last time we were there, our bill came in a little folder printed with three rules for the wise. If you're feeling the pressure and don't want to stop antiquing, I've included some good caffès where you can get a quick bite and keep going.

Antica Osteria L'Agania
Via Massini, 10
011-39-0577-253-81

Buca di San Francesco
Via San Francesco, 1
011-39-0575-232-71
www.bucadisanfrancesco.it

La Lancia d'Oro
Piazza Grande, 18
011-39-0575-210-33

CAFFÈS AND ICE CREAM
Caffè dei Costanti
Piazza San Francesco, 19
011-39-0575-216-60

Il Gelato
Via dei Cenci, 24
011-39-0575-232-40

Pasticceria Mignon
Via Tolletta, 20
011-39-0575-298-60

Regional Antiques Fairs
In addition to the many food markets throughout Tuscany, there are antiques and flea markets each month as well. They take place on the weekends, and you can happily spend every Saturday and Sunday foraging in markets with charming names like the "Little Dust Fair" or the "Fair of Trinkets." Below are some of the nicest ones and details of when they occur.

AREZZO
Throughout the entire town
The first Sunday of each month and the preceding Saturday
Foto Antiquaria
Piazza Grande
The last Sunday of April and September

CORTONA
City Center
The third weekend of each month

FLORENCE
Piazza Santo Spirito
The second Sunday of each month, closed July and August

Fortezza da Basso
The third weekend of each month, closed July and August

Piazza dei Ciompi
The fourth Sunday of each month, closed July

LUCCA
Piazza del Duomo
The third weekend of each month, closed July and August

PISA
Via Santa Maria
The second weekend of each month, closed July and August

SIENA
Piazza del Mercato
The third Sunday of each month, closed August

Antiques Shows
Biennale in Florence
Mostra Mercato Internazionale dell'Antiquariato
Palazzo Corsini
Via del Parione, 11
011-39-055-282-283
www.mostraantiquariato.it
The Biennale is one of the most prestigious international antiques shows in the world, on par with New York City's Winter Antiques Show and London's Grosvenor House. It alternates every other year between Florence and Paris, and occurs at the end of September. Usually held at one of the grand palazzos in town, like the Palazzo Corsini, it features an extravagant selection of priceless antiques from more than eighty international dealers. Experience the chic Florence arts and antiques scene at its most sophisticated.

Florence

The Perfect Center

"I was born in Florence many years ago. To be born in Italy and in Florence is good fortune: you have only to raise your eyes and Art and Beauty come to meet you."

—Franco Zeffirelli

Good fortune indeed. Florence was the artistic and cultural center of the magnificent period of the Renaissance, and flourished like no other place on earth during the fifteenth and sixteenth centuries. In her jewel of a book, *The Stones of Florence,* Mary McCarthy said, "The Florentines, in fact, invented the Renaissance, which is the same as saying that they invented the modern world." Today, you have only to raise your eyes to see a city bursting with the fruits of this artistic heritage.

Florence can seem like one enormous museum, with shadows of the great geniuses everywhere—works by the likes of architect Filippo Brunelleschi, sculptors Michelangelo, Donatello, and Luca Della Robbia, and painters Leonardo da Vinci, Raphael, Giotto, Botticelli, Cimabue, Fra Angelico, Masaccio, and Domenico Ghirlandaio. It has been celebrated by writers the world over, first by exceptional Florentines such as Dante, Boccaccio, and Petrarch and continuing with international literary luminaries including Goethe, Lord Byron, George Sand, Fyodor Dostoevsky, Robert and Elizabeth Browning, Rainer Maria Rilke, Henry James, Ralph Waldo Emerson, Henry Wadsworth Longfellow, and Mark Twain—just to mention a few. I could go on and on and on. There are thousands of books that cover the subject. If you want to know more or refresh your memory, see the Suggested Reading section.

Once you get there, you'll find that there are so many extraordinary things to see, it seems almost impossible to focus and decide what to do first. This overwhelming sensation actually has a name. It's called the Stendhal syndrome, named after the world-famous French novelist, who when visiting Italy completely lost his composure anticipating all the beauty he was about to see. Florence was too much, and the stricken Stendhal said: "I had palpitations of the heart . . . I walked with the fear of falling . . . my soul, affected by the very notion of being in Florence . . . was already in a state of trance." According to the Florentine tourist industry, some people still check into the city's hospitals suffering from an excessive exposure to art! (They say no Italian has ever complained of the problem!)

Like most people visiting this city for the first time, I too was overwhelmed by everything there was to see and do. I was there working in the fashion industry and since I had been an art major in college, I didn't know how I could possibly take it all in— much less appreciate it as I should. As I said in my last book, *A Passion for Antiques,* though things have changed—I no longer have a Mary Quant haircut or wear a miniskirt—I'm still in

OPENING PICTURE: I found this vintage fan in the Mercato delle Pulci in the Piazza dei Ciompi.
OVERLEAF LEFT: A birds-eye view of Brunelleschi's dome, atop the ornate Duomo, which is continually being restored and right, chocolates by your pillow in a little silver dish.
LEFT: The past and present unite at my favorite corner of the Borgo San Jacopo on the Oltrarno.

love with Florence all these years later. Like Lucy Honeychurch in E. M. Forster's novel, *A Room with a View,* the pernicious charm of Italy worked on me, and, instead of acquiring information, I began to be happy.

The city of Florence has been shaped by Tuscany's tumultuous history. The Roman settlement of Florentia was established by Julius Caesar in 59 BC. The endless conflicts between the Guelfs, who supported the pope, and the Ghibellines, who supported the emperor, went on for centuries, pitting city against city and marking the region forever. The Medici family came to power in the mid-fifteenth century in Florence, ushering in the Renaissance ideal of the "universal man" and an atmosphere of relative stability, productivity, and creativity lasting more than fifty years and never seen before or since.

Today Florence is a contrast of old and new, its outwardly stern and severe demeanor a perpetual contradiction to the hedonistic luxury of its glittering boutiques and opulent museums. It is a vibrant, cosmopolitan city inundated with tourists, who stand on ancient street corners unfolding their maps oblivious to the hazards of the speeding, noisy vespas whizzing by. I can't tell you everything you may want to know about Florence, but here are some practical points to keep in mind:

• Try to avoid this low-lying city in July and August, as both the temperature and humidity rise unpleasantly and tourism is at its peak.

Late fall (September and October) and early spring (April, May, and June) are especially lovely.

• Florence is a wonderful walking city with surprises at every turn; however, finding a particular street address can sometimes be confusing because of its idiosyncratic numbering system. Black or blue building numbers designate residences, while red numbers refer to businesses. This means that the same number can occur at different places on the same block. An "r" (for *rosso* or red), is usually printed after the street number on a business card or stationery, and the number will be painted red on the building. Ignoring this important detail could result in a long walk or expensive taxi ride. To further confuse the issue, some businesses, such as hotels, don't use the "r" at all.

• The Italian language is said to be spoken most perfectly in Tuscany. However, in Florence you may have difficulty understanding certain words, since the "c" is often pronounced as an "h," for example, "Hoca-Hola" for "Coca-Cola," or "hosa" for "cosa."

• Regarding opening and closing hours—as I've said before, remember this is Italy. Shop hours can change frequently, but a general rule is that they open between 8:00 and 9:00 AM and close between 12:30 and 1:00 PM for lunch, to reopen between 3:30 and 4:30 PM until 7:30 PM or so. Museums generally open at 9:00 AM and close at 1:00 PM, some reopen again at 4:00 PM

ABOVE: The bright red sightseeing bus in Florence, painted with its colorful artwork, contrasts with a somber ancient stone Renaissance palazzo on the Via dei Tornabuoni.

and some don't. If you have a tight schedule and do not want to be disappointed, check the times before you go. Pick up a free copy of "Florence Concierge Information" available at the reception desk of every hotel and tourist office. It lists up-to-date hours for museums, galleries, and churches in addition to current city cultural events and activities such as concerts, or antiques and garden shows. Everything closes for lunch. Lively streets previously thronged with people empty out and all one hears is the clanging of metal shutters being pulled down over shop windows. It's time to surrender yourself to a long, lovely lunch, then back to the hotel for a short siesta. To get the most out of visiting Florence, or indeed any place in Italy, adapt to the schedule of the locals. This means getting up early and doing as much as you can before lunch. Also, many stores are closed on Monday morning and do not open until 3:30 or 4:00 PM.

• Walking city or not, there are still times when you will need a taxi (after a shopping spree on the Via dei Tornabuoni perhaps). The taxi situation is amazingly organized. You can call one from anywhere in the city and they usually arrive within minutes. You can sometimes ask a shop to call one for you. We have used the company Radio Taxi Firenze (055-42-42) with great success.

Florence probably has more recognizable

landmarks than most cities. Over one hundred years ago D. H. Lawrence astutely wrote, "And in Piazza della Signoria he felt he was in one of the living centers of the world . . . he had reached a perfect center." The Piazza was originally the city's political center, and it still is a meeting place today, crowded with Florentines stopping to chat and a crush of photo-happy tourists—some taking the sun at Rivoire, one of the city's best-known caffès, some exploring the artworks in the treasure-filled square like the Loggia della Signoria, recently reopened after its sculptures were restored by the international organization Friends of Florence (see page 218).

The Palazzo Vecchio, the fortress-like city hall with its elegant interiors, and the Uffizi Gallery, with its fine collection of Renaissance paintings, are in the piazza near the spot where rebel preacher Girolamo Savonarola was burned for heresy in 1498. Today, most of the city's major events and rallies are held here with great pageantry. It's the perfect place to be in the evening when Florentines take a leisurely promenade (*passeggiata*) after dinner to catch up on the local gossip or just watch the world go by.

It's a short walk to some of the city's other main squares, like the Piazza del Duomo, with its awe-inspiring Cathedral of Santa Maria del Fiore and topped by Brunelleschi's famous dome (you can climb the stairs to the top).

Nearby is Giotto's elegant Campanile and the sublime Baptistery, Florence's oldest building, with its lavish doors designed by celebrated sculptors of the time, Andrea Pisano and Lorenzo Ghiberti. The famous east doors were called the "Gates of Paradise" by Michelangelo because they are so magnificent.

The Piazza della Repubblica was the site of the ancient forum in Florence. It's still a noisy spot. A children's carousel, several expensive outdoor caffès, and four or five groups of musicians all playing different tunes and surrounded by crowds enjoying the free show, are just some of the activities that take place here day and night.

The Piazza della Santissima Annunziata, off the beaten track at the end of the Via dei Servi, hosts many special city events like the colorful Feast of the Annunciation on March 25th and the Feast of the Rificolona in September. There's also a wonderful ceramics fair in October, which was noted in Chapter Four.

Piazza Santa Croce is a lively spot filled with visiting students and tours congregating on the church steps and outdoor stalls displaying everything from pottery, leather coats, and handbags, to souvenirs to buy. The Church of Santa Croce features Michelangelo's majestic tomb by Giorgio Vasari as well as those of Machiavelli, Galileo, and over two hundred other prominent citizens, plus a cycle of frescoes by Giotto and the Capella dei Pazzi by Brunelleschi.

ABOVE: Florence is a shopper's paradise where you can buy almost anything including these charming Pinocchios from street vendors.
BELOW: Soft leather gloves beckon from a shop window.

If you are in the mood for a nice walk, you can stroll from Santa Croce across the Arno River via the Ponte alle Grazie to the landmark Piazzale Michelangelo. If you don't feel like walking, it is a short taxi or bus ride (#12 or #13 from Ponte alle Grazie). This is where the many photographs of the beautiful views of Florence are usually taken—so be sure to take your camera. While you are there, visit the Church of San Miniato al Monte with its geometric green-and-white marble facade built in 1018 and the Giardino dell'Iris, planted in the 1950s as a tribute to the flower that has been Florence's symbol since 1251. Open only in May, it features more than 2,500 varieties of iris. Before you head back, stop for a cool drink or an espresso at one of the outdoor caffès in the piazza.

My favorite neighborhood in Florence has always been the Oltrarno (which means "over the Arno"). This district on the south bank of the Arno River was home to vineyards and olive groves until the Medici grand dukes moved there in the mid-sixteenth century. I love wandering its narrow streets and feeling that I am in a friendly small neighborhood similar to New York's Greenwich Village or the Left Bank of Paris.

Many talented artisans and craftspeople practiced their crafts on these winding, ancient streets for centuries—frame and furniture makers, woodcarvers, textile weavers,

metalworkers, and silversmiths—all creating and restoring some of the most beautiful objects that you will ever see. This neighborhood is also home to a group of sophisticated antiques shops. And if you are not a collector there are unique stores carrying everything from handmade clothing and accessories to hard-to-find olive oils and local gourmet specialties.

Two of the most important churches in Florence are here—Santa Maria del Carmine with its seminal frescoes by Masaccio in the precious Cappella Brancacci, and my favorite, the simple Church of Santo Spirito designed by Brunelleschi. This peaceful, pale yellow building is in the Piazza Santo Spirito, a market square where Florentines shop for fruits, vegetables, and household items daily, catching up on neighborhood gossip in the friendly caffès nearby. On the second Sunday of the month there's a terrific artisans craft market here, and on the third Sunday one featuring organic and local foods. Casa Guidi, where Robert and Elizabeth Browning moved after their secret marriage, is close by at no. 8 San Felice, and is open to the public on a limited schedule.

Just down the street is the majestic Pitti Palace. It houses several important museums that feature the private collections of the

LEFT, ABOVE: There is a special window in the private quarters of Palazzo Frescobaldi that overlooks the magnificent, elegant interior of the Santo Spirito Church.
BELOW: A gold florin from the jeweler Torini.

Medicis: the Galleria Palatina, with an extraordinary array of art and sculpture; the Museo degli Argenti, displaying fabulous silver, tortoise, shell, ivory, and mother-of-pearl objets d'art; and the Galleria delle Costume, with antique textiles, costumes, and clothing. Walk up to the top of the Boboli Gardens behind the Pitti Palace to a special museum, the Galleria delle Porcellane, which houses porcelain from the Medici and Lorraine dynasties. It's a secret spot with a special little garden (see Chapter Two) and views of the surrounding hillsides, unchanged since the Renaissance.

Oltrarno can be reached from the center of the city via several bridges, the most famous being the Ponte Santa Trinità and the Ponte Vecchio. The Ponte Vecchio has been lined with various shops since the thirteenth century. Initially they were butchers and food vendors, but in the sixteenth century the Medicis, as befitting their exalted position, replaced them with goldsmiths and jewelers, and their successors are still there today, working in the tradition of the fine goldsmiths of the past. In fact, Florentines were among the first to mint their own gold coin in 1252. It was called the florin and soon became the standard currency used in many parts of Europe, making Florence a banking power. (You can buy a beautiful gold copy at Torrini, the venerable jewelry store near the Duomo, to hang on a charm bracelet as a reminder of Florence).

The Ponte Vecchio is always jammed with students and visitors, many taking photographs from the bronze Benvenuto Cellini statue in the center. Despite its raffish atmosphere, it is still possible to find a treasure or two. On our honeymoon my husband bought me a necklace of Baroque pearls from U. Gherardi, a friendly, family-owned firm that specializes in coral and pearl. It is still located at no. 5, near Piccini, another jewelry shop I like that has been there forever.

The Corridoio Vasariano, which runs over the Ponte Vecchio, is a private shortcut, a passageway designed by Giorgio Vasari that the Medicis took from their office in the Uffizi to their home, Palazzo Pitti, to avoid going into the street. It has been restored, hung with portraits and paintings by the likes of Rubens and Raphael, and is now open to the public by reservation (see listings on page 164).

From the Ponte Vecchio you can see the next bridge, the Ponte Santa Trinità, designed in 1567. It is said that the respected architect Bartolomeo Ammannati showed his plans to Michelangelo for his approval because it was such an important commission. Destroyed during World War II, this graceful bridge has become a symbol of the proud Florentine citizens, who painstakingly rebuilt it exactly as it was. Today it mirrors the austere elegance and indomitable spirit of this historic city.

Hotels

I lived in Florence early in my fashion career, and my husband and I have been traveling to the city for decades. In those early days we frequented inexpensive youth hostels and pensioni. The first one I stayed in cost $8.25 a night, breakfast and dinner included! I only wish life was so simple today. We've stayed in all the hotels on this list. Some are more to our liking than others, but they all maintain a special level of service and decor. One caveat: Florence is a loud city, so if noise is an issue ask for a quiet room when making your reservation. Recently we had one memorable stay at the delightful Palazzo Niccolini al Duomo; with its majestic yet warm interiors, intimate atmosphere, and hospitable owners, we felt as though we were guests in someone's home.

Continentale
Vicolo dell'Oro, 6r
011-39-055-272-62
www.lungarnohotels.com
Very in, very modern.

Grand Hotel
Piazza Ognissanti, 1
011-39-055-288-781
www.starwoodhotels.com
An old favorite; reserve an elegant room overlooking the Arno.

Hotel Lungarno
Borgo San Jacopo, 14
011-39-055-272-61
www.lungarnohotels.com
Redone in chic Ferragamo style; ask for a room with a river view.

Hotel Savoy
Piazza della Repubblica, 7
011-39- 055-273-51
www.roccofortehotels.com
A Rocco Forte hotel, in the thick of things.

Palazzo Niccolini al Duomo
Via dei Servi, 2
011-39-055-282-412
www.niccolinidomepalace.com
Great location, great service.

Villa Antea
Via Puccinotti, 46
011-39-055-484-106
www.villaantea.com
Neoclassic, away from the crowds.

OUTSIDE THE WALLS
The following hotels are outside of the center city, ideal if you are visiting Florence in the summer and want to avoid the heat and the bustle. Try one of these beautiful hotels, each with its own distinctive look, impeccable service, and swimming pool.

Grand Hotel Villa Cora
Viale Machiavelli, 18
011-39-055-229-8451
www.villacora.it
Turn-of-the-century Italian style.

Torre di Bellosguardo
Via Roti Michelozzi, 2
011-39-055-229-8145
Beautiful views.

Villa La Massa
Via della Massa, 24
50012 Candeli, Florence
011-39-055-62-611
www.villalamassa.com
As elegant as its sister hotel, the Villa d'Este.

Villa La Vedetta
Viale Michelangiolo, 78
011-39-055-681-631
www.villalavedettahotel.com
Ultramodern decor, breathtaking views.

Villa San Michele
Via Doccia, 4
50014 Fiesole
011-39-055-594-51
www.villasanmichele.com
Where the rich and famous go to get away from it all.

Dining

We've had some extraordinary meals in Florence. Our preference is always for small trattorias with genuine Tuscan food made from local ingredients. Some of these restaurants are small, good, and always crowded, so remember to make a reservation. Many are closed on Sundays, so plan ahead. Here we've given you a range of the best of the best—from ice cream shops, caffès, and wine bars to the most sophisticated restaurants. Enjoy every delicious mouthful.

All'Antico Ristoro di Cambi
Via San Onofrio, 1r
011-39-055-217-134
www.anticoristorodicambi.it
Good, uncomplicated cooking.

Al Tranvai
Piazza Tasso, 14r
011-39-055-225-197
Trendsetting favorite.

Antica Fattore
Via Lambertesca, 1/3r
011-39-055-288-975
Old-fashioned, steps from the Uffizi.

Buca dell'Orafo
Volta dei Girolami, 28r
011-39-055-213-619
A favorite, tiny, near Ponte Vecchio.

Caffè Ricchi
Piazza Santo Spirito, 8r
011-39-055-215-864
Chic neighborhood favorite.

Cammillo Trattoria
Borgo San Jacopo, 57r
011-39-055-212-427
I ate here when I worked in Florence—delicious.

Cantinetta Antinori
Piazza Antinori, 3r
011-39-055-292-234
Palazzo setting, superb family wines.

Cibrèo
Via A. del Verrocchio, 8r
011-39-055-234-1100
Superstar Fabio Picchi's trendsetter.

Da Nerbone
Mercato Centrale di San Lorenzo
011-39-055-219-949
Inexpensive, but open only at lunch.

Da Sergio
Piazza San Lorenzo, 8r
011-39-055-281-941
Family-run, simple, and inexpensive.

Enoteca Pinchiorri
Via Ghibellina, 87
011-39-055-242-777
www.enotecapinchiorri.com
Formal, three Michelin stars.

Fuor d'Acqua
Via Pisana, 37r
011-39-055-222-999
Go Friday night for fresh seafood.

La Loggia
Piazzale Michelangelo, 1
011-39-055-234-2832
www.ristorantelaloggia.com
Incomparable view.

Nanamuta
Corso Italia, 35
011-39-055-267-5612
www.nanamuta.it
Pop in after the theater.

Oliviero
Via delle Terme, 51r
011-39-055-287-643
Modern, updated Tuscan food.

Omero
Via Pian de'Giullari, 11r
011-39-055-220-053
www.ristoranteomero.it
Good views, ten minutes from city.

Osteria del Cinghiale Bianco
Borgo San Jacopo, 43r
011-39-055-215-706
www.cinghialebianco.it
Delicious, friendly, always packed.

Pandemonio
Via del Leone, 50r
011-39-055-224-002
Family-run neighborhood trattoria.

Ristorante Il Guscio
Via dell'Orto, 49
011-39-055-224-421
A casual Florentine favorite.

Ristorante Sabatini
Via Panzani, 9a
011-39-055-282-802
Old-fashioned, elegant.

Trattoria Garga
Via del Moro, 48r
011-39-055-239-8898
www.garga.it
Contemporary art, good, interesting food.

Trattoria Nella
Via delle Terme, 19r
011-39-055-218-925
Touristy, but friendly and reasonable.

Trattoria 4 Leoni
Via dei Vellutini, 1r
011-39-055-218-562
www.4leoni.com
Very casual, outdoor seating.

Trattoria Zibibbo
Via di Terzollina, 3r
011-39-055-433-383
www.zibibbonline.com
Benedetta Vitali's delicious food.

CAFFÈS
Da Scudieri al Battistero
Piazza San Giovanni, 19r
011-39-055-210-733
Local favorite with a Duomo view.

Rivoire
Piazza della Signoria
011-39-055-214-412
Sit outside and dawdle over the legendary hot chocolate.

ICE CREAM
Gelateria Carabé
Via Ricasoli, 60r
011-39-055-289-476
www.gelatocarabe.com
Known for its Sicilian-style granitas.

BELOW: Florentines make some of the best gelato!

Vivoli
Via Isola delle Stinche, 7r
011-39-055-292-334
www.vivoli.it
Get in line with all of Florence—worth the wait.

WINE BARS

Cantinetta dei Verrazzano
Via dei Tavolini, 18r
011-39-055-268-590
Stylish sandwiches and wine.

Frescobaldi Wine Bar
Via de'Magazzini, 2-4r
011-39-055-284-724
www.frescobaldiwinebar.it
Hot spot featuring the family's wonderful wines.

Il Santo Bevitore
Via di Santo Spirito, 64r
011-39-055-211-264
For a quick bite on the Oltrarno.

Procacci
Via dei Tornabuoni, 64r
011-39-055-211-656
Have a truffle panini and prosecco thanks to the Antinoris, who saved this Florentine institution.

Museums

I have slanted my list toward small, lesser-known museums that have focused collections and are not thronged by crowds. I did include the classics such as the Uffizi, which though continually mobbed with tourists cannot be ignored because of the important treasures within. Note: most museums start to empty out in the late afternoon and some are open one night a week, so try to take advantage of this. If you want to avoid long lines for state museums (the never-ending line at the Uffizi Gallery comes to mind) you can reserve tickets by telephone then pick them up at the museum and receive a reservation number for the day

and time of your visit. A small reservation fee is charged in addition to the admission fee (011-39-055-294-883).

Bardini Museum
Piazza de'Mozzi, 1
011-39-055-234-2427
Fifteenth- to seventeenth-century eclectic treasures.

Bargello Museum
Via del Pronconsolo, 4
011-39-055-238-8606
The finest collection of Renaissance sculpture in the world.

Biblioteca Medicea Laurenziana
(Laurentian Library)
Piazza San Lorenzo, 9
011-39-055-210-760
A masterpiece by Michelangelo, next to the Church of San Lorenzo.

Cappella Brancacci (Brancacci Chapel)
Piazza del Carmine
011-39-055-238-2195
Tiny gem with seminal fifteenth-century frescoes by Masaccio.

Le Medicee (The Medici Chapel)
Piazza Madonna degli Aldobrandini, 6
011-39-055-238-8602
The amazing Medici mausoleum, with sculptures by Michelangelo.

Cloister of Santa Maria Novella
Piazza di Santa Maria Novella
011-39-055-210-113
Next to the important church, with frescoes by Paolo Uccello and the famous Farmacia with its fragrant soaps and potions.

Corridoio Vasariano (Vasari Corridor)
Uffizi Gallery
011-39-055-283-044
Covered passageway from the Uffizi to the Pitti Palace. By appointment.

Ferragamo Museum
Via dei Tornabuoni, 2
011-39-055-336-0456
Vintage shoes by Salvatore Ferragamo. By appointment.

Galleria dell'Accademia
Via Ricasoli, 60
011-39-055-238-8609
Michelangelo's masterpiece David *is here.*

Horne Museum
Via dei Benci, 6
011-39-055-244-661
Renaissance art and objects in a fifteenth-century palazzo.

La Certosa
Galluzzo
011-39-055-204-9226
Twenty minutes outside of Florence, this Cistercian monastery contains terracottas by the della Robbias and lunettes by Pontormo, and a shop featuring liquors and herbal remedies made by the monks.

Museo dell'Opera del Duomo
Piazza del Duomo, 9
011-39-055-230-2885
Contains astonishing treasures from the Duomo, construction materials used for Brunelleschi's dome, and a version of the Pietà by Michelangelo.

Museo Stibbert
Via Stibbert, 26
011-39-055-475-520
Frederick Stibbert's villa outside Florence, filled with important furniture, porcelain, pottery, arms, and armor.

Opificio delle Pietre Dure
Via degli Alfani, 78
011-39-055-265-1357
Established in 1588 by the Medicis, and dedicated to semiprecious stone inlays.

Palazzo Pitti (Pitti Palace):
011-39-055-238-8611
Galleria Palatina
Priceless Medici art collections, including my favorite miniaturist, Giovanna Garzoni.
Museo degli Argenti (Silver Museum)
Silver, mother-of-pearl, and ivory.
Museo delle Porcellana (Porcelain Museum)
Antique porcelain tableware.
Galleria del Costume (Costume Gallery)
Eighteenth- to twentieth-century fashion.

Uffizi Gallery
Loggiato degli Uffizi, 6
011-39-055-238-85
Designed by Vasari, see important Renaissance paintings in chronological order.

Shops

Shopping is one of Florence's chief pleasures, which is another reason I adore this city. I love shopping and am constantly updating my list. There are thousands of stores and open-air markets with lavish displays. I've tried to highlight ones with special merchandise that you can't find anywhere else—such as Loretta Caponi's luscious handmade linens and Old England, with everything for homesick expatriates from British gumdrops to Scottish tartans, both located on Via dei Tornabuoni.

I didn't include designer boutiques with branches in every major city of the world—you can easily shop in them at home. (I did include Pucci, because it is a renowned Florentine original and I couldn't live without it). And since this is the center of the universe for shoe lovers, I haven't listed any particular shoe stores, because I don't believe in preferential treatment. Over the years I've bought a pair of shoes in almost every shop in the city! My suggestion is to start at Ferragamo on Via dei Tornabuoni and go on from there (don't forget to make an appointment to visit the Shoe Museum at the top—a treat!).

You'll want to add the St. James Thrift Shop to your list, too. It's a treasure trove of clothes and household items open on the first Wednesday of each month. Rub shoulders with the locals while enjoying a cup of tea or coffee. The proceeds are shared by the worthwhile St. James Food Bank and the Missionary Sisters of Charity founded by Mother Teresa. It's located in the lovely St. James Church, "the American Church in Florence," founded in 1853 and located at Via Bernardo Rucellai, 9 (011-39-055-294-417).

ANTIQUES SHOPS
Most antiques shops are clustered in two areas: on Via Maggio in the Oltrarno and on Villa dei Fossi and Borgo Ognissanti near the Grand Hotel on the other side. Here is a short list of some favorites.

Antichità
Via dei Fossi, 7r
011-39-055-217-092

Antichità Piselli Balzano
Via Maggio, 23r
011-39-055-239-8029

Antonella Pratesi
Via dei Fossi, 7r
011-39-055-287-683

Bona Tondinelli Antichità
Via Maggio, 28r
011-39-055-284-060

Gallori-Turchi Antichità
Via Maggio, 14r
011-39-055-282-279

Giovanna Rizzi Antichità
Via Mazzetta, 15r
011-39-055-280-141

Giovanni Turchi
Via Maggio, 50-52r
011-39-055-217-341

Lambtons
Via Maggio, 69r
011-39-055-280-375

Lo Spillo
Borgo San Jacopo, 72r
011-39-055-293-126

Massimo Vezzosi
Via dei Fossi, 29r
011-39-055-294-549

Pandora Decor
Via Ghibellina, 101r
011-39-055-264-033

Zecchi
Via Maggio, 34r
011-39-055-293-368

BOOKS
BM Book Shop
Borgoggnissanti, 4r
011-39-055-294-575
A wonderful selection in English.

CRYSTAL
Locchi
Via Burchiello, 10r
011-39-055-229-8371
www.locchi.com
An institution.

HOME DECOR
Antico Setificio Fiorentino
Via L. Bartolini, 4r
011-39-055-213-861
www.anticosetificiofiorentino.com
Lustrous silk fabrics.

Baroni
Via dei Tornabuoni, 9r
011-39-055-210-562
www.baroni-firenze.com
Bed and bath accessories.

Castorina
Via Santa Spirito, 13r
011-39-055-212-885
www.castorina.net
Frames and wood doodads.

Dino Bartolini
Via dei Servi, 30r
011-39-055-211-895
Wonderful housewares.

Ducci
Lugarno Corsini, 24r
011-39-055-214-550
www.duccishop.com
Traditional Florentine crafts.

Flair
Piazza Scarlatti, 2r
011-39-055-267-0154
Chic contemporary decor.

Loretta Caponi
Piazza Antinori, 4r
011-39-055-213-668
Delicate lingerie and baby clothes.

Manetti e Masini
Via Bronzino, 125r
011-39-055-700-445
Artisanal ceramics.

Richard Ginori
Via Rondinelli, 17r
011-39-055-210-041
www.richardginori1735.com
Tableware par excellence.

Leopoldo Menegatti
Via Vigna Nuova, 78r
011-39-055-213-327
Mosaics.

Lugarno Details
Lungarno Acciaiuoli, 4r
011-39-055-2726-4095
Ferragamo's home design store.

Parenti
Via dei Tornabuoni. 93r
011-39-055-214-438
Accessories for the home.

Passamaneria Valmar
Via Porta Rossa, 53r
011-39-055-284-493
www.valmar-florence.com
Tassels, tassels, and more tassels.

T & T
Via de'Ginori, 2r
011-39-055-280-123
Fabrics, tablecloths, and pillows.

Ugo Poggi
Via Strozzi, 26r
011-39-055-216-741
Table accessories.

JEWELRY

Angela Caputi
Via S. Spirito, 58r
011-39-055-212-972
and
Borgo SS. Apostoli, 44
011-39-055-292-993
www.angelacaputi.com
Dramatic costume jewelry.

Tharros
Borgo SS. Apostoli, 28r
011-39-055-289-388
My favorite Renaissance copies.

Pomellato
Piazza Antinori, 8r
011-39-055-213-200
www.pomellato.it
The real thing—chic.

Torrini
Piazza Duomo, 10r
011-39-055-230-2401
www.torrinishop.it
Buy a florin for your charm bracelet.

U. Gherardi
Ponte Vecchio, 5r
011-39-055-211-809
Pearls.

LEATHER

Scuola del Cuoio
Via San Giuseppe, 5r
011-39-055-244-533
www.leatherschool.com
The Church of Santa Croce leather school; buy beautifully crafted handmade leather accessories and bags here.

LOTIONS AND POTIONS

Alessandro Bizzarri
Via Condotta, 32r
011-39-055-211-580
Old Florentine herbal remedies.

Lorenzo Villoresi
Via de'Bardi, 14
011-39-055-234-1187
Exquisite perfumes, custom-made.

Officina Profumo di Santa Maria
Novella
Via della Scala, 16
011-39-055-230-2437
Still the best soaps and scents.

PAPER GOODS

Antica Baccani
Via Porta Rossa, 99r
011-39-055-215-448
Nice people, pretty paper.

Giulio Giannini & Figlio
Piazza Pitti, 37r
011-39-055-212-621
We love the paper here.

Pineider
Piazza della Signoria, 13r
011-39-055-284-655
www.pineider.it
Buy your engraved stationery here.

PASTRY SHOPS

Dolci e Dolcezze
Piazza Beccaria, 8r
011-39-055-234-5458
The best pastry shop in Florence.

READY-TO-WEAR ACCESSORIES

Alfreda e Manuela Evangelisti
Borgo dei Greci, 33r
011-39-055-292-772
Ties and scarves.

Bemporad
Via Calzaiuoli, 11r
011-39-055-216-833
Loden coats.

Emilio Pucci
Via dei Tornabuoni, 20r
011-39-055-265-8082
www.pucci.com
Need I say more?

Ferragamo
Via dei Tornabuoni, 14r
011-39-055-292-123
www.ferragamo.com
Shoes, handbags, and ready-to-wear.

Old England Stores
Via Vecchietti, 28r
011-39-055-211-983
Scottish tartans to Burberry.

Roberto Ugolini
Via Michelozzi, 17r
011-055-39-216-246
Custom-made shoes.

Stile Biologico
Via dello Sprone, 25r
011-39-055-277-6275
www.stilebiologico.it
Environmentally friendly fabrics.

Ugolini
Via dei Tornabuoni, 20r
011-39-055-216-6644
More gloves.

Zuffanelli
Via dei Lamberti, 1r
011-39-055-239-6174
www.zuffanelli.it
My favorite scarves and shawls.

SHIPPERS

Mail Boxes
Lungarno Guicciardini, 11r
011-39-055-212-002
Very helpful and fast.

SILVER

Brandimarte
Viale L. Ariosto, 11cr
011-39-055-230-41
www.brandimarte.com
Silver and silver plate.

Paolo Pagliai
Borgo San Jacopo, 41r
011-39-055-282-840
Impeccable craftsmanship.

Pampaloni
Borgo SS. Apostoli, 47r
011-39-055-289-094
The place to register for wedding silver.

SEEDS AND GARDENS

Morganti
Piazza Santo Spirito, 3r
011-39-055-289-230
Italian seeds and garden accessories.

Al Portico
Piazza S. Firenze, 1r
011-39-055-213-716
www.semialportico.it
Baskets, beans, and seeds.

ABOVE: It's fun to bring home seeds from Italy, in this case, Italian fennel, parsley, and basil.

TUSCAN FOOD SPECIALTIES

I Sapori del Chianti
Via dei Servi, 10r
011-39-055-238-2071

La Bottega dell'Olio
Piazza del Limbo, 2r
011-39-055-267-0468

Oleum Olivae
Via S. Egidio 22/r
011-39-055-200-1092
www.oleum.biz

Olio & Convivium
Via Santo Spirito, 4r
011-39-055-265-8198
www.conviviumfirenze.it

To Market, to Market

Open-air markets are a tradition in Florence and some have been around for hundreds of years. Called barroccini, *which means "carts with wheels," they were the forerunners of Florence's shops and department stores.*

FOOD MARKETS

These markets reflect the Tuscan focus on good food. The selection of mouthwatering produce, meats, fish, and cheeses from all around Tuscany are featured here. With its friendly vendors and boisterous atmosphere, it's a wonderful overview.

Mercato Centrale di San Lorenzo
Via dell'Ariento, 10—14
Monday to Saturday, 7 AM to 2 PM
The largest in Florence, this active food market is in a cavernous nineteenth-century cast-iron building. Stop in at Nerbone for the Florentine specialty tripe, and at the friggitore, Via di Sant'Antonio, 50r, for deep-fried donuts and savory snacks.

Mercato di Sant'Ambrogio
Piazza Sant'Ambrogio
Monday to Saturday, 7 AM to 2 PM
This important market is favored by the Florentine *cognoscenti* because of its good selection of organic produce.

Fierucoline di Santo Spirito
Piazza Santo Spirito
Third Sunday each month
This is a totally organic market selling everything from homemade soaps to cheeses and traditional Tuscan breads.

∾ ∾ ∾ ∾ ∾ ∾

ABOVE: Colorful hydrangeas for sale every Thursday.
RIGHT: A tourist attraction in the Piazza della Repubblica.

GENERAL MARKETS

If you love shopping, you'll love the following markets. They sell a bewildering selection of colorful Italian silk scarves and shawls, leather goods, and gift items. If you have a good eye, you can find some wonderful buys. And do bargain—it's expected.

Mercato Nuovo, or Straw Market
Loggiato del Porcellino
9 AM to 7:30 PM daily
This market is open during lunchtime and is handy from almost anyplace in Florence. Rub the nose of the *porcellino*, the brass boar, for good luck.

Mercato di San Lorenzo
Piazza San Lorenzo
9 AM to 7:30 PM daily
Go from one end to the other to find touristy and sometimes chic gifts to bring home.

∾ ∾ ∾ ∾ ∾ ∾

FLOWER MARKET

Every Thursday stalls selling plants and flowers are set up in the shade of the loggia that runs alongside the Piazza della Repubblica.

Mercato delle Piante
Loggiati di Via Pellicceria
Thursday, 8 AM to 5 PM

∾ ∾ ∾ ∾ ∾ ∾

ANTIQUES MARKETS

The antiques markets are fun because you mingle with the locals and can sometimes find a treasure or two, but I would save my big bucks for the fabulous antiques show in Arezzo (see pages 148–149 for details).

Mercato di Santo Spirito
Piazza Santo Spirito
Second Sunday of each month
Under the trees, a fun market with the occasional find.

Mercato delle Pulci
Piazza dei Ciompi
First Sunday of each month
Can be hit or miss, you might find some interesting collectibles.

SEVEN

The True Tuscany

Discovering the Essence

"Italy gives much, in beauty, gaiety, diversity of arts and landscapes, good humor and energy—willingly, without having to be coaxed or courted."

—Kate Simon

T U S C A N Y

Massa

Lucca

A11

Pisa

Florence
Fiesole
Settignano

S.Casciano
Impruneta

Montifiridolfi

Livorno

Greve
Panzano
A1

S2
A11
Radda

San Gimignano
Gaiole
Castellina

Colle di Val d'Elsa
S222

Monteriggioni

Arezzo

Pievescola
Siena

S2

Bolgheri
Sinalunga
A1

Cortona

Carducci
San Galgano
Monte Oliveto Maggiore

Buonconvento
Pienza
Montepulciano

S. Vincenzo
San Quirico
Montichiello

Montalcino
Chianciano Terme

Castiglione D'Orcia
Bagno Vignoni
Chiusi

Sant Antimo
S2
Cetona

Piombino

Protoferraio

Grosseto

Castiglione della Pescaia

ELBA
Sorano

Saturnia
Sovana

Pitigliano

Porto Ercole
Monte Argentario

Isola del Giglio

This lovely thought from Kate Simon is how we often feel when going about our everyday life in Tuscany. There is something beguiling about a place that encourages you to do the impulsive rather than the planned, to appreciate simplicity, to wander, to linger, to savor the moment— *la dolce vita*. Tuscany is like that.

This chapter is about the Tuscany my husband and I love, the Tuscany that we've traveled since we were just starting out in the fashion business many years ago. It's not my intention to create a complete travel guide. There are loads of books available today, not to mention the Internet, offering laundry lists of information. Instead we've focused on an edited selection of "insider" places, as well as the special "finds" suggested by Italian friends and all the wonderful people we met along the way while working on this book. These are the spots we recommend to our good friends when they call for advice.

Our choices feature lesser-known places that are authentic and less touristy, in addition to some old favorites that are more well-known. Also included are the hotels and restaurants that have made our many trips to Italy so memorable, plus some new discoveries. As a shopaholic, I was compelled to include some of the luscious shops that are in every Italian city—bastions of style, taste, and sometimes wonderful bargains.

Some things to keep in mind: Tuscany is a comparatively small region and most of the towns and villages are fairly close to one another, which almost creates its own itinerary because in many cases you must go through one little town to reach the next. We have organized this chapter by natural progression, so you don't miss anything.

Many towns, built on hilltops, are happily off-limits to cars. You must park in the small spaces provided outside the town gates and (sometimes unhappily) walk up steep hillsides. Remember that usually everything but restaurants will be closed for two to three hours in the afternoon. Line up a good place for lunch to revive and relax like the locals.

There are several good highways (*autostrada*, *superstrada*, etc.) that will quickly get you from one end of Tuscany to the other. We prefer the winding country roads that generally have very little traffic. Although they are lightly traveled, most of the time they tend to have clearly marked road signs, even in out-of-the-way places. Exploring the rural back roads often will result in lovely, unexpected adventures, some of the fondest memories of your trip—a field of bright red poppies, the tranquil ruins of a long-forgotten chapel, a friendly outdoor caffè in the middle of nowhere filled with people enjoying a sunny day. To happily travel through Tuscany, leave time for surprises—just drive and let something wonderful happen.

OPENING PICTURE: Grapes and olives growing in the Chianti hills around Badia a Passignano.
OVERLEAF LEFT: After many years the "new mill" still survives and, right, guidebooks in many languages.
LEFT: A simple map of Tuscany marked with the major routes and the towns mentioned in this chapter.

Chianti

The gentle vine-clad Chianti hills between Florence and Siena are the home of the famous Chianti Classico wines. The Etruscans introduced vine growing to this land in the third century BC, and it continues to be the beating heart of the region. The landscapes depicted in some of the masterpieces of the Renaissance capture the serene lushness and mystique of the picturesque castles, farmhouses, medieval villages, and hill towns that dot a landscape that has remained unchanged for centuries. Driving on the famous Via Chiantigiana (Chiantigiana Road) road, S 222, which runs north and south through the region, is a journey through time.

This is a land of plenty: grapes, olives, corn, chestnuts, and lavender are just some of the local crops that grow in profusion. The enthusiasm for food and wine attracts people from all over the world. In fact the British have been going to this area for so long that it is often humorously called Chiantishire. In the midst of summer, certain parts can become crowded, so you need to plan ahead.

Greve in Chianti

Greve, the "little capital of Chianti," is a bustling market town near the old Chiantigiana road, eighteen miles from Florence. It's an easy day trip but there's so much to do here and in the surrounding towns that you can easily run out of time. We usually try to stay over at Fonte de'Medici, one of the good local *agriturismos* that is centrally located, which gives us a chance to leisurely explore this rich wine center of Tuscany.

Greve is the heart of the Chianti Classico region, that includes over six hundred wine growers. Their symbol is the Gallo Nero, a black rooster that represents the consortium of Chianti Classico wine makers. You'll see the black, red, and white emblem everywhere you go. There is a huge wrought-iron sculpture of the black rooster in front of the parking area in Greve where you should leave your car. Then it's just a two-minute walk to the heart of town, the triangular Piazza Matteotti.

Dominating the square is the imposing Palazzo Comunale and in the center is a statue of Giovanni da Verrazzano, who is credited with discovering the New York harbor. Behind it is the neoclassical Church of Santa Croce, which boasts a fifteenth-century triptych of the *Madonna and Child with Four Saints* by Bicci di Lorenzo. It's quiet in the church but not in the square, because its covered porticos feature a mixture of touristy souvenir kiosks, fine shops, food stores, *enotecas*, and restaurants that always seem to be busy.

There's always something wonderful to do in Greve. Wine and harvest festivals abound in September; Rassegna del Chianti Classico, the most important wine fair, occurs in the middle of the month and should not be missed. Every Saturday morning there's an outdoor market featuring fresh produce and flowers from the surrounding countryside. An antiques show occurs twice a year, usually in April and October, and Lamole, a small village nearby, holds a music festival every summer.

There are so many wonderful places to buy the good regional wines and olive oils that it's impossible to include them all here. One thing you can do is to go to the Chianti Classico consortium website (listed below) for helpful wine information. It lists all the high-quality wineries in the region, including details for each and whether they do wine tastings, sell olive oil, and the like.

You can easily spend several hours in the Piazza Matteotti and the streets that radiate from it. There are some outstanding wine stores, and several small shops in which I always find amazing hand-embroidered linens and children's clothes. Be sure to visit the renowned Antica Macelleria Falorni, established in 1782, and admire the prodigious displays of traditional homemade *prosciutto, finocchiona*, and *salsicce*.

Tuscan Notes ⌒ GREVE IN CHIANTI

RESTAURANTS
Ristorante Giovanni da Verrazzano
Piazza Matteotti, 28
011-39-055-853-189
www.ristoranteverrazzano.it
Sit upstairs for the view.

Ristorante Il Portico
Piazza Matteotti, 83
011-39-055-854-7426
Simple good food.

HOTELS
Fonte de'Medici
Via Santa Maria a Macerata, 31
50020 Montefiridolfi
011-39-055-824-4700
www.fontedemedici.com
See Chapter One.

SHOPS
Antica Macelleria Falorni
Piazza Matteotti, 69-71
011-39-055-853-029
Traditional salami and sausages.

Biancheria Fantechi
Viale Giovanni da Verrazzano, 25
011-39-055-854-376
Embroidered linens.

Giachi Grazia Ricami
Piazza Matteotti, 35
011-39-055-854-4671
Embroidered linens.

L'Inganno di Sophie Rose and Nell Rose
Piazzetta Santa Croce, 2
011-39-055-853-431
Home décor.

La Pizzicheria
Silvano & Franca
On the Piazza
011-39-055-853-541
The place for picnic food.

WINE STORES
Bottega del Chianti Classico
Via Cesare Battisti, 2-4
011-39-055-853-631

Enoteca del Chianti Classico
Piazzetta Santa Croce, 8
011-39-055-853-297

Le Cantine di Greve in Chianti
Galleria della Cantine, 2
011-39-055-854-6404
www.lecantine.it

CONSORZIO DEL MARCHIO STORICO-CHIANTI CLASSICO
Via Scopeti, 155
50026 San Casciano Val di Pesa
011-39-055-822-85
www.chianticlassico.com
This organization located just north of Greve represents the best of the Chianti Classico producers, and their helpful website lists fine vineyards to tour, wine tastings locations, and locally produced olive oils. Enjoy wandering the countryside, stopping at as many congenial places as possible to explore, sample the local bounty, and make some new discoveries to bring home.

Panzano

This little gem of a village is on a ridge 1,600 feet above sea level, just south of Greve. You can easily visit both in the same morning. Panzano is on two levels, so on entering take the first right, a narrow little road that goes up past a group of special shops and luxurious villas set behind lush gardens.

On your way up, you should make two stops. On your left is Carlo Fagiani's, where you can leave your car in the tiny space in front. He makes luscious leather clothing and handbags, and my favorite, made-to-measure shoes. Imagine an entire wall of soft leather shoe samples that you can have custom-made in any style or color under the sun: hot pink, turquoise, chartreuse, citron yellow, bright red, and yes, basic black and navy, too. The best news is the reasonable prices. If you can't get back in a week or so, they will send them to you. Next walk across the street to a small hardware store that has a special array of iron handles, hooks, hasps, and assorted hand-wrought goodies to give your house that Tuscan look.

Drive on to the top and one of my favorite churches, the twelfth-century Church of Santa Maria Assunta. Before you climb up the steep steps, enjoy the facade and contemporary sculptor Umberto Bartoli's bas-relief portrait of the Madonna surrounded by angels over the bronze doors. Then take a peak inside the brick structure, which was transformed in the neoclassical style during the nineteenth century.

The panoramic views of the Pesa Valley on the way down are camera-worthy. The rest of the town at the bottom has some interesting shops. Antica Macelleria Cecchini is the chicest butcher shop I've ever seen. Baskets of beautiful vegetables and the aroma of fresh herbs and spices surround the various meats. The shop is owned by Dario Cecchini, who has become a legend after years spent enthusiastically promoting authentic Tuscan cuisine. You'll be invited to sip a glass of Chianti and listen to soft music while waiting for your order—add this to your list of unique Tuscan experiences.

One of the best-preserved churches in the Chianti area is here—the Church of San Leolino. It boasts a Romanesque facade and houses many beautiful early paintings and frescoes, a triptych by Mariotto di Nardo, and two tabernacles by Giovanni della Robbia.

Tuscan Notes ∼ PANZANO

SHOPS

Antica Macelleria Cecchini
Via XX Luglio, 11
011-39-055-852-020
macelleriacecchini@tin.it
A wonderful butcher.

Carlo Fagiani
Via Giovanni da Verrazzano, 17
011-39-055-852-239
www.carlofagiani.com
Custom-made shoes.

Luca Dainelli
Via Giovanni da Verrazzano, 48-50
011-39-055-852-115
Wrought-iron hardware.

Castellina in Chianti

Years ago, we rented a house in Tuscany with a group of friends, and the first weekend there we decided to explore. We ended up having a delicious lunch and afternoon in Castellina in Chianti, a wonderful way to start a vacation. Plan to visit when you are in this part of the country, as Castellina is a just a short drive from Panzano or Radda.

This town dates from Etruscan times, and remains of a necropolis (Etruscan cemetery) from the seventh century B.C. can be found in the nearby towns of Fonterutoli and Monte Calvario. Castellina's history is tumultuous because of its location between Florence and Siena. In the fifteenth century, it was rebuilt with the stone walls that define it today. In fact there are stone buildings everywhere, including the ancient fortress that dominates its skyline—the fifteenth-century Rocca Comunale, now the town hall.

As is the case in most of these hill towns, you must park your car at the base of the town and enter on foot. Try to park near the entrance of the Via Ferruccio, where shops, exceptional wine stores, and *enotecas* line both sides of the street. The dramatic facade of the Palazzo Ugolini Squarcialupi, which is now a hotel, is halfway down. Stop in the sixteenth-century neo-Romanesque Church of San Salvatore, which contains many Renaissance treasures. It was rebuilt after being damaged during World War II. From almost any vantage point atop Castellina, you can look out to see grapes and olives growing as far as the eye can see. In mid-summer (July, August, and even September), the town can be crowded, but it's always worth a visit, if only for the wonderful bottles of olive oil and wine to choose from in the open-air market that is held every Saturday in the lovely town square.

Tuscan Notes ❧ CASTELLINA IN CHIANTI

RESTAURANTS
Osteria alla Piazza
La Piazza Castellina
011-39-0577-733-580
Good food.

Trattoria La Torre
Piazza del Comune, 15
011-39-0577-740-236
Family favorite.

HOTEL
Hotel Palazzo Squarcialupi
Via Ferruccio, 22
011-39-0577-741-186
In the center of town.

SHOPS
Lucia Volentieri
Via Trento e Trieste, 24
011-39-0577-741-133
Creatively designed ceramics.

Pep Bizzarrie
Via Trento Trieste, 12
011-39-0577-740-738
www.pepbizzarrie.it
Cute pottery gifts.

Toscanaccio Antichità
Via Ferruccio, 44
011-39-0577-742-930
Stylish selection.

WINE STORES
Bottega del Vino
Piazza del Comune, 13
011-39-0577-741-110
www.enotecadelchianti.it

La Castellina
Via Ferruccio, 26
011-39-0577-740-454

Le Volte Enoteca
Via Ferruccio, 12
011-39-0577-741-314

Radda in Chianti

We like Radda, an intimate spot in the heart of Chianti Classico country. This medieval town, which sits at the top of a ridge, basically has three levels: the major road you will arrive on; the level above, a street called Via Roma; and the lane behind it, which winds back down and offers one of the prettiest views of the surrounding hills. You can leave your car at the bottom of the main road near the Hotel Relais Vignale, which is a good place to stay for those who want to be in the center of it all. It's well run, has two restaurants, a sleek wine store, and a hillside pool with views of the vineyards.

Radda has an interesting history, and in the thirteenth century it was the center of the Chianti League, a distinguished club of landowners who grew and made wine. The narrow Via Roma leads to the civic building, the Palazzo Pretorio, with its distinctive facade adorned by the heraldic plaques of the chief magistrates dating from the 1200s. Along with some nice shops, bars, and food stores, half-way up the hill is a wonderful fourteenth-century church, San Nicolò. After the uphill climb through the town, you will arrive at a little piazza at the top. Turn left, and on the way down follow the medieval stone wall for a panoramic view of the slopes of Monte dei Chianti.

This town should win a Chamber of Commerce award, because the shop owners are so friendly and accommodating. Our camera broke the last time we were there, and the man in the hardware store repaired it—and wouldn't accept any money. There is also a group of talented artisans in Radda. Silvia and David Matassini own pretty Neltempo, an Aladdin's cave of treasures for the home featuring one of their specialties, the ancient technique of *marmorino*, a method of fresco painting that has been revived from the fifteenth century.

I love the pottery at Ceramiche Rampini, especially the sophisticated tableware that features Tuscan farmyard animals cavorting on a blue, white, and yellow background. It's located just a couple of miles from town on the road to Gaiole in Chianti. That's where Badia a Coltibuono, the world-renowned cooking school and winery, is located (see page 119).

Be sure to have lunch at Ristorante Le Vigne, and sit outside drinking wine from the vineyards below and water from their very own spring that is served in cobalt blue bottles.

PREVIOUS PAGE LEFT: Near Pienza we encountered a surprise—this field of bright red poppies.
PREVIOUS PAGE RIGHT: Candid photos taken as we wandered through the countryside including, top, the butcher in the market in Montalcino; the family dog snoozing at Badia a Coltibuono; and below, the facade of Santa Maria Assunta in Panzano.
RIGHT: A view of the beautiful hills from Panzano.

HOTELS

Fattoria Castello di Volpaia
Localita Volpaia
011-39-0577-738-066
info@volpaia.com
Twelfth-century chic.

Relais Vignale
Via Panigiani, 9
011-39-0577-738-300
www.vignale.it
In the heart of town.

RESTAURANTS

La Cantoniera di Vescine
Route 429
011-39-0577-741-195
Very pretty.

Osteria di Volpaia
Piazza della Cisterna, 1
011-39-0577-738-066
www.volpaia.com
Perennial favorite.

Ristorante Le Vigne
Podere Le Vigne
011-39-0577-738-640
Eat outdoors on the hillside.

SHOPS

Arrighi Antichità
Via Pozzo dei Birri, 1
011-39-0577-738-504
Antique décor.

Ceramiche Rampini
Casa Beretone di Vistarenni
011-39-0577-738-043
Beautiful, handmade selection.

Chianti Cashmere Company
Azienda Agricola La Penisola
011-39-0577-738-080
www.chianticashmere.com
Creamy soaps and shampoos.

Francesco Rossi
Via Roma, 40
011-39-0577-738-075
Cute kitchen accessories.

La Bottega delle Fantasie
Via Roma, 30
011-39-0577-738-978
Luscious cashmere throws.

Neltempo
Silvia & David Matassini
Viale G. Matteotti, 1
011-39-0577-738-158
www.decorineltempo.it
Chandeliers, ceramics, and murals.

Terrecotte Barbieri
Viale XX Settembre, 7
011-39-0577-738-773
Terracotta pottery.

WINE STORES

Caparsino
Azienda Agricola Caparsa
011-39-0577-738-639
www.caparsa.it

ABOVE: A special view over the varied, textured rooftops of Siena featuring the Torre del Mangia.

Siena

Siena is a city of fine Gothic architecture, the Palio, and *panforte*. According to legend, it was established in the Roman era by Senius, son of Remus, which accounts for images of Romulus, Remus and the she-wolf on Siena's emblems and flags. Despite its conflicts with Florence, many of its important buildings from that era have survived.

Like most hill towns, Siena does not allow cars in the center, so you must park outside the city walls. To save walking extra steps up its steeply narrow streets, consult a good city map before you set out and decide which entrance is nearest your destination. We park at the garage closest to the center of town, just outside the Porta Fontebranda near the Piazza San Domenico.

Surrounded by four and a half miles of medieval walls, today Siena looks much as it must have in the sixteenth century—except for the crowds of tourists that sometimes overwhelm it. You can see the city from miles around, because it's perched on three hilly ridges called *terzi*. Because of this, the streets crisscross each other in confusing ways.

The three hills converge at the scallop-shaped Piazza del Campo, the heart of the city. It is one of the most famous squares in Italy, and we usually stop to have a quick espresso here. Dominating it is the Palazzo

Pubblico, Siena's town hall, the model for many of the other city palaces. It's worth a visit, and its beautiful interiors are filled with collections of paintings, ceramics, and silver from the twelfth to nineteenth centuries. Alongside is the Torre del Mangia, a tower built in the 1300s, offering lovely views of the city. The nearby Pinacoteca Nazionale, in the Palazzo Buonsignori, is home to many impressive paintings by the artists who worked in Siena during the Renaissance.

Of course one can never mention Siena without discussing the colorful Palio. Held in the Piazza del Campo, the Palio has fascinated people from all over the world since the thirteenth century. The Palio is a historic race with neighborhood teams competing in traditional costumes on horseback, galloping at top speed around the square to earsplitting cheers. A fiercely competitive event with feasts, parades, and parties, it is held twice each summer—on July 2nd, (the day of the Madonna di Provenzano) and August 16th, which is the day after the Ferragosto, another important holiday in Italy.

Those in the know arrive days in advance to enjoy the spectacle and the activities leading up to the actual event: a dress rehearsal, many processions, and the blessing of the horses in the churches. After the race, the victorious neighborhood or *contrade* wins a silk banner symbolizing their victory and bragging rights for the next year. If you wish to view the Palio in style, you can arrange it with the owners of some of the many *palazzi* overlooking the square like Palazzo d'Elci, built in 1200 (see Tuscan Notes).

Don't miss the Piazza del Duomo and the distinguished Cathedral of Santa Maria Assunta, whose dramatic facade of white, green, and red marble was created by Giovanni Pisano. Begun in 1229, it wasn't completed for another hundred years. You can easily spend hours inside its amazing interior, which includes geometric bands of cream and green/black marble and magnificent floors paved in colored marble inlay.

Opposite the Duomo is the impressive Santa Maria della Scala, a hospital since the eleventh century that was in use until just a few years ago, when it became a museum. Now its underground passages house a stunning archaeological collection spanning ten centuries of rare Greek and Roman antiquities.

As with Florence, there is so much of interest to art and architecture buffs that before you visit obtain a good guidebook that will put you in the picture. If you collect antiques there are pretty shops to tempt you and an antiques show on the third Sunday of each month in the Piazza del Mercato.

Enoteca Italiana—headquartered in one of the oldest meeting places in Siena, the

Fortezza Medicea built by Cosimo de'Medici—is a boon for the wine enthusiast. This organization promotes the region's many wines and has over 1,000 available for tasting. It's also an information center where you can learn about the history of wine, buy a bottle of your favorite vintage, and even have a snack in the cantina. It also sponsors events such as Settimana dei Vini (Wine Week), usually held in June, and Settimana Nazionale dell'Olio (Olive Oil Week), in February.

Everyone looks forward to market day in Siena. Each Wednesday stalls are set up around La Lizza near Piazza Gramsci, where the freshest produce is available at the area's largest market. The city is home to many food stores featuring Sienese specialties such as *panforte* (a flat cake made of candied fruits and nuts) and *riccarelli* (light, almond cookies), and although it is said that its restaurants are not necessarily the best, we've listed some that we have enjoyed over the years.

Some towns around Siena have become so crowded that it is no longer fun to visit them, except off-season. Years ago we had the best lunch in San Gimignano and strolled through the charming town, viewing Domenico Ghirlandaio's fresco of *The Annunciation* in an almost empty Duomo. Last year we had to skip it, because there were tour buses everywhere and it was impossible to find a place to park.

That said, we still love the surrounding countryside and always stop at the Fattoria San Donato on San Gimignano's outskirts. It is an old farm that looks like a medieval village directly out of central casting with old painted grape carts and giant green glass wine bottles leaning on stone walls. The large Fenzi family welcomes you to their wine or olive oil tastings, and you can have a friendly chat and even buy a few bottles of wine or oil to take home with you. Nearby is the Lotti Paolo terracotta factory that has large burnt-sienna colored pots in a variety of antique designs and a nice selection of tabletop and kitchenware. They stock oversized shapes that are difficult to find and, good news, they ship!

Abbey of San Galgano

On SS 73 between Siena and
Massa Marittima
Chuisdino
011-39-0577-756-738

Nestled in the Sienese countryside sits the silent, thirteenth-century Abbey of San Galgano built by Cistercian monks from Rome. By the sixteenth century, the building was a roofless ruin—nonetheless it is still powerful and hauntingly impressive. It was built in honor of Galgano Guidotti, later Saint Galgano, and the rock in which he planted his sword in 1180 is still there. The cathedral is a majestic series of archways leading from one end to the other. There is also a hermitage, the domed church of San Galgano sul Monte Siepi, which contains notable frescoes by Ambrogio Lorenzetti.

Tuscan Notes ✍ SIENA

HOW TO SEE THE PALIO
Palazzo d'Elci
Countess d'Elci
011-39-0577-280-820
cesarinadelci@virgilio.it

RESTAURANTS
Antica Trattoria Botteganova
Via Chiantgiana, 29
011-39-0577-284-230
Outside of town, but worth it.

Bagoga
Via della Galluzza, 26
011-39-0577-282-208
Quietly refined.

Cane e Gatto
Via Pagiaresi, 6
011-39-0577-287-545
Cozy restaurant, good food.

Da Guido
Vicolo Pier Pettinaio, 7
011-39-0577-280-042
Typical Sienese meeting place.

Il Ghibellino
Via dei Pellegrini, 26
011-39-0577-288-079
Locals eat here.

Osteria Nonna Gina
Pian dei Mantellini, 2
011-39-0577-287-247
Mama Gina is in the kitchen.

CAFFÈS
Nannini
Via Banchi do Sopra, 22/24
011-39-0577-236-009
Touristy but fun.

SHOPS
Dolci Trame
Via del Moro, 4
011-39-0577-461-68
Wonderful ready-to-wear.

Drogheria Manganelli
Via di Città, 71
011-39-0577- ? -?
Tuscan food specialties since 1879.

Fioretta Bacci
Via San Pietro, 7
011-39-0577-282-200
Handmade scarves and sweaters.

Tesori di Siena
Via di Città, 72
011-39-0577-467-23
Artisan designed; they will ship.

ANTIQUES
Antichità L'Accademia
Via di Città, 77
011-39-0577-491-93
Beautiful old jewelry.

Antichità Monna Agnese
Via di Città, 45/99
011-39-0577-282-288
Nice selection.

Antiquariato Taddeucci
Via di Città, 136
011-39-0577-289-160
Worth a stop.

Saena Vetus
Via di Città, 53
011-39-0577-423-95
vasco@comune.siena.it
Good taste.

Il Restauro
Siena-Grosseto Superstrada
011-39-0577-385-866
Nice furniture.

ENOTECAS
Enoteca Italiana
Via Camollia, 72
011-39-0577-228-811
www.enoteca-italiana.it

BELOW: The Tuscans treasure old farm pieces that have been around their farm for centuries like this colorful wagon at Fattoria San Donato.

NEAR SAN GIMIGNANO:

WINES
Fattoria San Donato
Località San Donato, 6
53037 San Gimignano
011-39-0577-941-616
www.sandonato.it
Wine and olive oil.

SHOPS
Lotti Paolo
Località Capannino Fosci
53037 San Gimignano
011-39-0577-942-019
Terracotta for the garden.

Dreaming of Tuscany 187

Monteriggioni

Around Siena, we often head north to two nearby towns, Monteriggioni and Colle di Val d'Elsa. Viewed from a distance crowning the top of a gentle hill, Monteriggioni looks as it did when Dante wrote in his *Divine Comedy* of "Monte Riggion with towers crowned." This small village has a church and several dozen houses, neatly encircled by a fortified wall with fourteen square towers, a rare example of medieval military architecture that protected it from the time it was built in the early twelfth century.

It's always nice to stay close to the places that you intend to visit. Sumptuous La Suvera, a favorite hotel and resort (see Chapter Five), is close to Siena, so when we stay there we sleep late, take a leisurely swim, and plan on a delectable lunch in Monteriggioni at Ristorante Il Pozzo. People come from far and wide to dine here, so you must reserve—a table outside is a treat if the weather is nice. On Thursdays, you can check out the weekly outdoor market. After lunch, take a short *passeggiata* through town and go in to the lovely Romanesque-Gothic Church of Santa Maria Assunta on the tiny main square.

Tuscan Notes ∽ MONTERIGGIONI

RESTAURANTS
Ristorante Il Pozzo
Piazza Roma, 2
011-39-0577-304-127
www.ilpozzo.net
Deserves its fine reputation.

SHOPS
Opera di Maria Albenico
Via 1 Maggio
011-39-0577-306-058
Well-made reproduction jewelry

Tuscan Notes ∽ PIEVESCOLA

HOTEL
Relais La Suvera
53030 Pievescola
011-39-0577-960-300
www.lasuvera.it
Simply divine.

BELOW: A charming terrace with a stunning view.

ABOVE, LEFT: Everyone has to have a coffee break, especially in Italy, and right, terracotta pots in every style and size are stacked outside an artisinal factory near San Gimignano.

Colle di Val d'Elsa

Colle di Val d'Elsa lies just a few miles away. There are two parts to this artisanal town. The industrial lower part, called Colle Basso, is the site of glass manufacturing that creates 90 percent of the fine lead crystal made in Italy. Here, master craftsmen blow and engrave glass according to traditional methods developed long ago. You can still visit some of the workrooms and purchase samples.

Colle Alta, the medieval part of town, clings to a rocky spur above and has some fascinating ancient buildings. It boasts of being the birthplace of architect Arnolfo di Cambio, who designed the historic Palazzo Vecchio and Santa Croce in Florence. On the main street, Via del Castello, you'll find the Palazzo Priori, now the Museo Civico e d'Arte Sacra; the Palazzo Pretorio, home to the Bianchi Bandinelli Archaeological Museum; and at number 63, the watchtower that is said to be Cambio's birthplace. The seventeenth-century Duomo was restored in 1992.

Tuscan Notes ✍ COLLE DI VAL D'ELSA

RESTAURANTS
L'Antica Trattoria
Piazza Arnolfi di Cambio, 23
01-39-0577-923-747
Innovative cuisine.

Ristorante Arnolfo
Via XX Settembre, 50
011-39-0577-920-549
www.arnolfo.com
Two Michelin stars, great food.

SHOPS
Arnolfo di Cambio
Pian dell'Olmino
011-39-0577-928-279
www.arnolfodicambio.com
Fine crystal.

Consorzio Cristallo di Colle Val d'Elsa
Via di Castello, 33
011-39-0577-924-135
A group of glass stores.

Mezzetti Cristallerie
Via Oberdan, 13
011-39-0577-920-395
www.cristalleriemezzetti.com
Good crystal selection.

Terracotta Tesi
Località Pain dell'Olmino
53034 Colle di Val d'Elsa
011-39-0577-928-130
Wonderful splatterware pottery.

Val D'Orcia

Below Siena in southeastern Tuscany is a region of relatively undeveloped countryside that was recently designated a UNESCO World Heritage Site. This wide open valley of gentle green hills is planted with dark rows of cypresses that contrast with the Crete Senesi, the chalky clay fields that distinguish this area. Incredibly, some of the same views that enchanted the Renaissance painters still remain, almost untouched, today.

We really enjoy exploring this peaceful part of rural Tuscany, because it is much less crowded than places closer to the larger cities. Everywhere you turn are little towns, each of which has its own distinctive personality. There is a feeling that everything here is still authentic, and that new discoveries are to be made around every corner. The ancient abbeys of Sant'Antimo and Monte Oliveto Maggiore cast a magical spell over the tranquil countryside.

Majestic Monte Amiata, Tuscany's highest peak, rises out of the hills here, and its springs of crystal-clear water nurture the luxurious local vegetation, which results in delicious pecorino cheeses, fine honeys, and the world-famous wines of the region, Brunello di Montalcino and Vino Nobile di Montepulciano.

We usually head south from Siena on the route marked SS 2, the Via Cassia. This is one of the most revered ancient routes in Italy, following the old Roman road between Siena and Rome. Here are some of the places we always visit along the way.

BELOW: Summer is the time when Tuscans fill their famous window boxes with glorious color.

Buonconvento

We have friends who live in this small farming village just off the SS 2. It's encircled by fourteenth-century crenellated stone walls, and there is an entrance and parking lots at either end, so you can easily leave your car. One main street bisects the town and winds under a succession of arches that connects the surrounding walls.

Today, Buonconvento lives up to its hospitable name. We always have an espresso at the local caffè where much of the town congregates, or, if our timing is right, a delicious lunch at Mario's, a simple trattoria that has been run by the same family for years. The Museo d'Arte Sacra della Val d'Arbia and the Church of Santi Pietro and Paolo are worth a visit, but it's fun to just poke around town. There are some lovely shops and a busy outdoor market every Saturday morning. If you are there at Easter there's a four-day antiques fair, and the last week of September is reserved for the lively Val d'Arbia arts and music festival.

Tuscan Notes ∾ BUONCONVENTO

RESTAURANTS
Osteria da Duccio
Via Soccini, 76
011-39-0577-807-042
Unpretentious, good food.

Ristorante da Mario
Via Soccini, 60
011-39-0577-806-157
Friendly trattoria, good food.

ART GALLERY
The Gallery
Via Soccini, 1 A
011-39-347-143-4036
Wonderful paintings of Tuscany.

SHOPS
Artelier
Piazza Matteotti 8/10
011-39-0577-806-413
Stylish clothes and gifts.

Il Cantiniere Ghiotto
Via Soccini, 44
011-39-0577-809-032
Local food specialties.

Susy Laboratorio Artiginale
Via Soccini, 49
011-39-0577-807-079
Handmade accessories.

Monte Oliveto Maggiore

Localita Chiusure
011-39-0577-707-611
email: monteoliveto@ftbcc.tin.it
If you have time, take a small detour on the SS 451 from Buonconvento to the superb Monte Oliveto Maggiore. The pink-toned monumental abbey has been home to Benedictine monks since the fourteenth century, and today they specialize in restoring old books and making wine, honey, and olive oil. The remarkable Renaissance masterpiece, thirty-six frescoes of the life of Saint Benedict painted by Luca Signorelli and Sodoma, and the intricate wood choir stalls, circa 1503 by Fra Giovanni da Verona, are just two of the abbey's many extraordinary treasures. There is also a restaurant and a shop where you can buy some of the homemade products.

Montalcino

Just south of Buonconvento, turn right and travel about ten miles to the strategically perched hill town of Montalcino, home to the legendary Brunello di Montalcino. Each time you turn your head, there is a breathtaking vista of the Sienese landscape and Mount Amiata.

We always try to hit Montalcino on Friday, which is market day. Park outside the town, near the thirteenth-century Rocca, or fort, which houses Enoteca La Fortezza, the place to taste almost all the wines grown here. Nearby are stalls selling everything from ribbons and T-shirts to local pork sausages. And let's not forget the wine. Brunello di Montalcino was developed in the nineteenth century by the Biondi Santi family, who owned the oldest vineyards in the area. Now Brunello is produced by many estates that you can tour. Some, like Villa Banfi, even have stylish restaurants on their properties.

There's so much to do in Montalcino, especially if you are a food or wine aficionado. During the summer and fall there are many food festivals: Settimana del Miele (honey week) is held at the beginning of September; chestnuts and mushrooms are celebrated the last Sunday in October; and of course a fuss is made over the white truffles in November, when they are sold at a market in nearby San Giovanni d'Asso.

The town is built on a medieval plan with attractive squares and buildings linked by cobbled streets. There are many enotecas where you can sample a glass of the local harvest. Food emporiums are abundantly stocked with local products including artisanal cheeses, olive oil, honey, and sweets. Don't overlook the Church of Sant'Agostino with its Romanesque facade and rose window. Next door is the Civic and Diocesan Museum, which houses prehistoric and Etruscan remains.

Sant'Antimo

Castelnuovo dell'Abate
53024 Montalcino
011-39-0577-835-659

You will gasp with pleasure when you first see this peaceful Benedictine abbey that sits in a valley six miles south of Montalcino. They say that Charlemagne founded Sant'Antimo in the ninth century. After lying abandoned for many years, today this graceful, light-filled building is home to French Cistercian monks, who celebrate the mass with Gregorian chants morning and evening. To add to the allure, legend has it that Charlemagne planted tarragon here, and to this day it is the only place in Italy where this herb is grown. There is also a sweet gift shop with handmade soaps, creams, and carved wooden objects made by the monks.

LEFT: This view from La Foce, featured in Chapter Two, is just a sample of what you will see in this breathtaking part of southern Tuscany.

RESTAURANTS

Alle Logge di Piazza
Piazza del Popolo, 1
011-39-0577-846-186
Caffè and wine bar.

Caffè Fiaschetteria Italiana 1888
Piazza del Popolo, 6
011-39-0577-849-043
www.fiaschetteriaitaliana.it
Belle époque caffè.

Enoteca La Fortezza
Piazzale della Fortezza
011-39-0577-0577-846-147
www.enotecalafortezza.it
Sample great wines here

Enoteca Osteria Osticcio
Via Matteotti, 23
011-39-0577-848-271
Excellent wine bar.

Osteria le Potazzine
Piazza Garibaldi, 10
011-39-0577-846-054
Simple, local dishes.

Ristorante Boccon di Vino
Via Traversa dei Monti
011-39-0577-848-233
www.bsur.it/boccondivino
Dine on the outdoor terrace.

OUTSIDE OF TOWN

Il Castello/Taverna Banfi
Localita Sant'Angelo
A Poggio alle Mura
011-39-0577-816-054
email: ristorante@banfi.it
Sumptuous.

Osteria del Vecchio Castello
Poggio Alle Mura
Pieve di San Sigismondo
011-39-0577-816-026
Beautiful and elegant.

Poggio Antico
Localita I Poggi
53024, Montalcino
011-39-0577-848-044
www.poggioantico.com
Refined, creative dining.

WINE AND GOURMET FOOD

Bacchus
Via G. Matteotti, 15
011-39-0577-847-054
enotecabacchusmontalcino@yahoo.it
Slow food delicacies.

Enoteca di Giannetti Gigliola
Piazza Garibaldi, 6
011-39-0577-849-418
email: enoteca@montalcinoproduce.it
Good wine and oil.

Enoteca di Piazza
Piazza Garibaldi, 4
011-39-0577-849-194
email:info@enotecadipiazza.com
Wine, oil, and honey.

Enoteca Grotta del Brunello
Costa Garibaldi, 3
011-39-0577-847-177
email: grottadelbrunello@tin.it
Wine, sweets, and grappa.

Pasticceria Mariuccia
Piazza del Popolo, 29
011-39-0577-849-319
www.pasticceriamariuccia.it
Mouthwatering pastries.

SHOPS

Ceramiche Il Coccio
Via Matteotti, 20
011-39-0577-846-088
email: piamos@virgilio.it
Beautiful handmade designs.

La Sfinge
Costa del Municipio, 4
011-39-0577-846-062
Home décor.

Castiglione d'Orcia

On the road from Sant'Antimo to the next town, San Quirico d'Orcia, you will drive past several tiny villages that are worth stopping at. Castiglione d'Orcia is a hamlet on Mount Amiata dominated by the triangular Piazza il Vecchietta, which is paved with large stones and bricks. Above it is Rocca Aldobrandeschi, which is a terrific location for photographs of the panoramic views of Amiata and the Orcia Valley.

Bagno Vignoni

A huge, rectangular pool almost 150 feet long replaces the typical central square in this sunny hill town. Built during the time of Lorenzo the Magnificent, it has contained bubbling hot springs since the time of the Etruscans—even Saint Catherine of Siena is said to have enjoyed its therapeutic qualities, and there is a loggia at one end dedicated to her. Surrounding the pool are ancient buildings, many of travertine marble. The most striking is a palace by

Bernardo Rossellino built for Pope Pius II, whose coat of arms is on the facade.

Tuscan Notes ⌐ **BAGNO VIGNONI**

RESTAURANTS
Osteria del Leone
Piazza del Moretto
011-39-0577-887-300
www.illeone.com
Cordial, outdoor dining.

SHOPS
Hortus Mirabilis
Piazza delle Sorgenti, 35/A
011-39-0577-888-944
Herbal lotions and potions.

San Quirico d'Orcia

During the Middle Ages, this ninth-century town was an important stop for pilgrims traveling on foot from as far away as Canterbury, England. It sits on the old Via Francigena, the main route from the north to the holy site of Rome. It is notable for its twelfth-century fortified walls, magnificent gates, and its main church, the Romanesque Collegiata, whose elaborately carved portals are decorated with bas-reliefs and sculptures.

Inside the church is a fine rose window and the *Madonna and Child with Saints*, a triptych created expressly for the town in the fifteenth century by the Sienese painter Sano di Pietro. If you like Italianate gardens, visit the Horti Leonini, dating from 1581. Its formal area is planted with geometric boxwood parterres and rose bushes, and in the center is a statue of Cosimo de'Medici by Bartolomeo Mazzuoli sculpted in 1688. It is a lovely place to sit and ruminate on all the beautiful things you have seen.

Pienza

This gem of a town is called the "ideal city." It was designed in 1459 by Bernardo Rossellino, at the request of Enea Silvio Piccolomini—known as Pope Pius II, humanist, poet, and native son.

Four streets form a cross around the main brick-paved square, called Piazza Pio II, with a well in its center. Surrounding are buildings worth a visit, including the Duomo, the Bishop's Palace, the Palazzo Pubblico, and the Palazzo Piccolomini, which features a *giardino secreto* that offers a view of the countryside (see Chapter Two). The city is so picturesque that Franco Zeffirelli filmed *Romeo and Juliet* here, and it was in director Anthony Minghella's memorable movie *The English Patient*. Have lunch at his favorite trattoria (and ours, too), Latte di Luna, where we always have their handmade spaghetti with mushrooms and their special, *semifreddo*, hazelnut ice cream.

Outside the ramparts of Pienza are several streets delightfully renamed over one hundred years ago to reflect peace rather than war. You can stroll down the Via della Fortuna (fortune), Via dell'Amore (love), Via del Bacio (kiss), and (if you dare) the Via Buia (darkness).

This is a very special place with one food store after another displaying the richness of the region and the famous sheep's cheese, *pecorino*, which in Italy is synonymous with Pienza. Leave your car at the Porto al Prato, walk through to the Corso Il Rossellino, where all the shops are.

Tuscan Notes ~ PIENZA

RESTAURANTS

Il Rossellino Pienza
Piazza di Spagna
011-39-0578-749-064
Small and simple.

Ristorante Dal Falco
Piazza Dante Alighieri, 3
011-39-0578-748-551
Authentic dishes.

Trattoria Latte di Luna
Via San Carlo, 2/4
011-39-0578-748-606
Dine outdoors under the umbrellas.

HOTELS

Il Chiostro di Pienza
Corso Il Rossellino, 26
011-39-0578-748-400
Restored convent in the town center.

SHOPS

Altroieri
Corso Il Rossellino, 8
011-39-0578-755-107
Antiques.

Antichità Beatrice Caratelli
Corso Il Rossellino, 3/5/7
011-39-0578-748-775
Magnificent jewelry and glass.

Colombini
Corso Il Rossellino, 45/47
011-39-0578-748-771
Embroidered linens.

La Bottega del Cacio
Corso Il Rossellino, 66
011-39-0578-748-713
Gourmet food.

La Bottega del Naturista
Corso Il Rossellino, 16
011-39-0578-748-081
Slow food purveyor.

La Cornucopia
Piazza Martiri della Libertà, 2
011-39-0578-748-150
Beautiful selection of cheeses.

L'Enoteca di Ghino
Via del Leone, 16
011-39-0578-748-057
www.enotecadighino.it
Nice selection of wines.

Marisa Gonzi
Piazza Martiri della Libertà, 5/6
011-39-0578-748-395
ceramichegonzi@libero.it
Handmade ceramic pieces.

Nannetti & Bernardini
Corso Il Rossellino, 81
011-39-0578-748-506
Artisanal meats and cheeses.

Zazzeri
Corso Il Rossellino, 6
011-39-0578-749-145
Gourmet food; they will ship.

Montechiello

After Pienza head on to Montepulciano known for its fine architecture and outstanding churches. We take the back roads—dusty white pebbled lanes called *strade bianchi* that wind through fields planted with bright red poppies in the spring and golden wheat in the summer. There are no people for miles and miles, and the scenery is absolutely luscious, with the occasional medieval ruin, or elegant row of cypresses.

Montechiello is off the beaten track. About three hundred people live in this walled village famous for its crooked watchtower. We always stop to buy more of the creamy bed and table linens handwoven and sold by Fidia Cappelli in her tiny shop. Each July the town presents its Teatro Povero di Montechiello, unique plays written about and performed by the villagers.

Nearby is La Foce, which I've written about several times. It's so close that you must stop at this impeccably maintained garden (see Chapter Two).

Tuscan Notes ~ MONTECHIELLO

SHOPS

Fidia Cappelli
Via de Mezzo
011-39-0578-755-002
Linen shop.

THEATER

Teatro Povero di Montechiello
011-39-0578-755-118

GARDENS

La Foce
Strada della Vittoria,. 61
53042 Chianciano Terme
011-39-0578-691-01
www.lafoce.com

Montepulciano

This hill town, considerably larger than those surrounding it, is of great historical importance. Its elevated position between two valleys, the Val d'Orcia and the Val di Chiana, was long bitterly contested for by Siena and Florence. In the sixteenth century it was ceded to Florence, which sent architect Antonio da Sangallo the Elder to remodel many of its buildings, resulting in the stately Renaissance city we see today. It is a popular destination and can become crowded on the weekends and in the summer. Parking may be difficult to find; we try to leave our car as close as we can in the little parking lot near the lowest part of town, the Piazza Sant'Agnese.

After entering the gates, you'll be on the principle street, the Corso, which steeply ascends the length of the town, zigzagging to the top. Take a peak inside the Church of Sant'Agnese and marvel at its fourteenth-century frescoes, then continue up the Corso passing ancient Renaissance palaces, including Palazzi Avignonesi, Tartugi, and Buccelli. You'll arrive at Piazza Grande, the dramatic main square, also designed by Sangallo. Some of Montepulciano's most important buildings are here: the Palazzo Comunale, the fifteenth-century town hall with a tower you can climb for some sensational views, and the Duomo with Taddeo di Bartolo's altarpiece, *The Assumption*, and *The Alter of the Lilies*, by della Robbia.

On the second weekend of every month antiques, artisanal crafts, and gifts abound at the outdoor flea market on the square. Once you finish exploring the Piazza Grande, continue walking to the upper part of town. The view from the top is simply spectacular—on a clear day you can see Lake Trasimeno in Umbria.

Aside from the outstanding buildings and the masterpieces they hold, another reason to visit Montepulciano is to learn more about one of Italy's first DOCG wines, the highly esteemed Vino Nobile di Montepulciano (for more information, see the website listed below). The shops that line the Corso feature some of the best enotecas and wine stores in the area; don't forget a visit to the Consortium Wine Shop in the Palazzo del Capitano. If you are visiting the last Sunday in August, enjoy the Bravio delle Botti, Montepulciano's famous wine festival. It starts with a procession, followed by a barrel race up the steep streets, and ending with a great outdoor banquet. Cantine Aperte occurs in mid-May, when most wine cellars open for tastings. Finally, every Thursday there is an outdoor market with fresh local produce. As you leave town, be sure to stop on the outskirts at the exquisite Church of San Biagio—built of golden stone and set at the end of an avenue of dark green cypress trees.

RESTAURANTS

Antico Caffè Poliziano
Via di Voltaia Corso, 24/29
011-30-0578-758-615
Have hot chocolate here.

L'Acquacheta
Via del Teatro, 22
011-39-0578-758-443
Cute.

La Grotta
Localita San Biagio, 15
53045 Montepulciano
011-39-0578-757-479
Good food.

HOTELS

La Chiusa
Via della Madonnina, 88
53040 Montefollonico
011-39-0577-669-668
www.ristorantelachiusa.it
Good restaurant and hotel.

WINE SHOPS AND BARS

Enoteca Borgo Buio
Via Borgo Buio, 10
011-39-0578-717-497

Enoteca Incontri Nobili
Via San Donato
011-39-0578-757-919

Enoteca Oinochoe
Via Voltaia del Corso, 84
011-39-0578-757-524

SHOPS

Caseificio di Silvana Cugusi
Via della Boccia, 8
011-39-0578-757-558
formaggicugusi@libero.it
Famous cheese maker.

Macelleria del Corso di Arnaldo Binarelli
Via Voltaia nel Corso, 7
011-39-0578-757-025
An amazing butcher.

Consorzio del Vino Nobile di
Montepulciano
Piazza Grande, 7
011-39-0578-757-812
www.consorziovinonobile.it
You can learn more about the region's wine production and taste the varieties here. Check their website for details.

Chianciano Terme, Chiusi, and Cetona

Near Montepulciano are three towns worth seeing: Chianciano Terme, Chiusi, and Cetona. Chianciano Terme has been a thermal spa since 1005, when the Etruscans and Romans took advantage of its therapeutic qualities. You might want to take the waters too in this old-fashioned spa town. The pleasant hotels offer spa services, and there are some beautiful parks and a historic center that includes the aptly named Civic Archaeological Museum of Water.

Lovely Chiusi was an important Etruscan town, and many of its treasures now reside in its National Archaeological Museum, where you can sign up for a tour of the catacombs and Etruscan necropolis. Old choir books illustrated with miniatures of the Abbey of Monte Oliveto Maggiore are displayed in its unique Cathedral Museum. Cetona has recently experienced its own renaissance as a desirable second home location for the trendy, rich, and famous. It's a simple town but sophisticated people come here to dine at La Frateria di Padre Eligio, a restaurant known for its delicious food.

Tuscan Notes ✍ CETONA

Convent La Frateria
La Frateria di Padre Eligio
Convento di San Francesco
011-39-0578-238-261

BELOW: The famous hot springs pool in Bagno Vignoli surrounded by stone walls and buildings.

Cortona

Cortona—known as the Mother of Troy and the Grandmother of Rome—is one of Italy's most ancient towns. Archaeological treasures are still being unearthed today from the remarkable large funeral mounds known as Meloni del Sodo, in the Etruscan burial grounds of the wealthiest families. It's only about two hours from Florence, but many visitors do not get there, although it has become more popular since being featured in the best-seller, *Under the Tuscan Sun*.

The approach to Cortona is by a narrow road that winds past a magnificent domed Renaissance church, Santa Maria delle Grazie, that should not be missed. The town rests atop a hill from which you can see the plains of the Valdichiana and even Lake Trasimeno in the nearby region of Umbria. Park outside the city gates. Once you enter, walk up the steep, shop-lined streets toward the town square.

Several treasures should not be missed. The Museo Diocesano contains the famous *Annunciation* by Fra Angelico and paintings by native sons Luca Signorelli and Pietro Lorenzetti. The Accademia Etrusca displays Etruscan and Roman artifacts. The tiny Church of San Niccolò is among the many worth visiting.

These places are within walking distance of the Piazza della Repubblica, the town square, where everyone congregates during the day and takes their *passegiata* after dinner. The curving streets that radiate from it feature interesting shops crammed with an abundance of antiques, gourmet food, elegant table linens, gifts, and handmade ceramics. If you have time, stop for lunch or stay over at the stylish hotel, Il Falconiere, just a few minutes away. Its kitchen has a Michelin star and they offer cooking lessons (see page 120).

Tuscan Notes ⁓ CORTONA

RESTAURANTS
La Locanda nel La Loggiato
Piazza Pescheria, 3
011-39-0575-630-575
Simple food, terrific views.

Preludio
Via Guelfa, 11
011-39-0575-630-104
Good, traditional cuisine.

HOTELS
Locanda dell'Amorosa
Sinalunga
011-39-0577-677-211
www.amorosa.it
A charming fourteenth-century village turned into a hotel.

Relais Il Falconiere
Localita S. Martino 370
Cortona
011-39-0575-612-679
www.ilfalconiere.com
You can see Cortona from this hotel.

ANTIQUES
Antichità di Dragoni Daniela
Via Nazionale, 47
011-39-0575-630-277
An eclectic collection.

Antichità Marri
Via Nazionale, 36
011-39-0575-631-108
Lots of small antiques.

Antichità Rachini
Piazza della Repubblica, 7
011-39-0575-603-562
They have wonderful taste.

SHOPS
Le Telerie Toscane
Piazza Pescheria, 2
011-39-0575-631-212
Nicely designed linens.

Molesini
Piazza della Repubblica, 3
011-39-0575-625-44
www.molesini-market.com
Local gourmet foods and wine.

Maremma

Explore the Maremma to see another side of Tuscany—one that is sparsely settled, almost untouched by tourism. Located in the southernmost corner of the region, it stretches along the western coast of the Tyrrhenian Sea, a one-hour drive south from Siena and two hours' north of Rome.

The Maremma is an intriguing mixture of sandy beaches, rolling meadows, and dense inland forests where boar and wild horses still roam. When we arrive, we like to head to the beach. Although most of Italy's seaside towns lack the sophistication you find in other European countries, lovely undeveloped beaches here allow you to spend the day enjoying the smell of sea air and the gentle sound of the water.

The word *maremma* means marshes or swampy coast. The region was settled by the earliest Etruscans, but in the Middle Ages seawater invaded the lowlands, creating a marshland. Mosquitoes proliferated and malaria plagued the region. They say that Caravaggio died near here in 1610 from malaria. Reclamation efforts began in the late eighteenth century, but dramatic change occurred in the 1930s when the government stepped in and started clearing and draining the marshes, culminating in the 1950s.

This relatively unspoiled environment attracts nature lovers of all kinds: many people explore the region by bicycling, hiking, walking, or even horseback riding. Maremma is home to an amazing variety of plants and animals. Its several natural parks include the Parco Regionale della Maremma, south of Grosseto with flourishing wildlife that can only be visited on foot by a limited number of people each day.

Horseback riding is a tradition in the region. Maremma is jokingly called the "wild west" of Italy because of the *butteri*, Italian equestrian herdsmen (real cowboys) who tended the white Maremman cattle in the nineteenth century. Capalbio, a city known for its horse breeding, holds a fair every October and celebrates the few remaining herdsmen who still practice it.

Today Maremma is a prosperous region whose reclaimed marshlands are planted with wheat and sunflowers, wild herbs, olive orchards, and lush vineyards. In fact the first of the super-Tuscan wines, Sassicaia, was created here. The way to enjoy Maremma is to slowly explore the unspoiled countryside, visiting the medieval hamlets, Etruscan sites, mineral spas, and beaches while appreciating the bounty of wild game and seafood in some of the top restaurants in Tuscany.

RIGHT: Two views of the Maremma from the sea to the mountains. ABOVE: The dramatic underground pools at Grand Hotel Tombolo and below, vineyards surrounded by dramatic mountains.

Bolgheri

Turn off the Via Aurelia and drive down the three-mile avenue enclosed on both sides by a famous long row of stately cypress trees (2,540 to be exact). This impressive sight was celebrated by Italian poet Giosuè Carducci—known by every schoolchild in Italy—in his famous poem *Davanti San Guido*.

At the end of the allée is the charming village of Bolgheri, with its turreted gates, elegant archway, and restored castle. Gourmet food stores and restaurants line its cobbled streets, and there are outstanding views of the countryside. It's a perfect place for a lazy lunch at Osteria Magona, with its simple, local cuisine.

We head on to the Antinori family's 2,400 acre private wine estate, Tenuta Guado al Tasso. We were welcomed by Allegra Antinori who grew up here with her two sisters. The Antinoris are one of the royal families of Tuscany's wine tradition for twenty-six generations. The business was handed down from one male-dominated generation to the next, but now Allegra and her two sisters, Albiera and Alessia, are taking over under the guidance of their doting father Piero.

The sisters' connection with Maremma goes back to their childhood. Actually it goes back even further, because the girls' grandmother was a della Gheradesca; this noble family has been producing wine in Maremma since the seventeenth century, and Allegra told us that Bolgheri's streets are named after family members—but only their first names!

Tenuta Guado al Tasso is a magical spot, extending from the sea to the slopes of the hills behind it, where the traditions of Maremma are being continued. Vineyards, wheat, sunflowers, and olives surround the recently built winery and the Macchia del Bruciato, a 175-acre farm started by the Antinoris to protect breeds of endangered farm animals such as Tuscany's native Cinta Senese pigs. In the morning, we left our guest quarters to watch the children gathering warm eggs from the henhouses.

Just ten minutes away is the thalasso therapy resort Grand Hotel Tombolo. It is on the sea and has a grotto of saltwater pools. The sleek spa offers every state-of-the-art beauty and relaxation treatment in addition to a well-equipped gym. Leaving Bolgheri, take the Strada del Vino, or the "Etruscan Wine Trail," to the village of Castagneto Carducci, named after the poet and a museum that celebrates his life and work.

The next stop is one of the best restaurants in Italy: Gambero Rosso, located in a seaside villa in the summer resort of San Vicenzo. Fulvio Pierangelini and his wife Emanuela focus on fresh ingredients, obtaining their meat, poultry, and vegetables from local farms, the game from hunting preserves, and of course the best of the day's catch. The wine list is legendary, not only for its excellent selection but also for its reasonable prices. Pierangelini has said, "The more people enjoy wine, the more they enjoy my food." Reservations are a must.

RESTAURANTS
Gola e Vino
Largo Nonna Lucia, 2
011-39-0565-762-045
Dine outdoors in the summer.

Osteria Magona
Piazza Ugo, 2-3
011-39-0565-762-173
Simple Mediterranean cuisine.

REGIONAL PARK
Parco Regionale della Maremma
Via del Bersagliere, 7/9
58100 Alberese
011-39-0564-407-098
www.parcomaremma.it

RESTAURANTS
Ristorante Il Gambero Rosso
Piazza della Vittoria, 13
011-39-0565-701-021
Always special.

HOTELS
Grand Hotel Tombolo
Via del Corallo, 3
57024 Marina di Castagneto Carducci
011-39-0567-745-30
www.grandhoteltombolo.com
Indulge yourself.

Elba

After lunch in San Vicenzo, drive down to Piombino where you can catch the ferry to Elba, the largest of the islands off Tuscany, one mile off the coast. The ferry arrives at Portoferraio, the main harbor and capitol of Elba, where iron has been mined for three thousand years. Most people know Elba because Napoleon was exiled there for ten months in 1814. You can visit his house, the Palazzo dei Mulini, which still has some of his furnishings, books, and an interesting garden. Elba is one of the more popular holiday spots in the Mediterranean for families because of its nature preserves and hiking. You can just visit it for the dayand have a nice lunch at La Barca in Portoferraio.

RESTAURANTS
La Barca
Via Guerrazzi, 60-62
011-39-0565-918-036
Fresh seafood.

ABOVE: An elegant entrance to the town of Bolgheri.

ABOVE: Two spectacular views of the glistening sea from Hotel Il Pellicano in Monte Argentario.

Pitigliano, Sorano, Sovana, and Saturnia

These four towns lie close to each other—the first three built breathtakingly high into rocky tufa cliffs, to which they have been literally clinging since the Middle Ages. Pitigliano rests on a rampart between several river gorges; the carved grottoes at its base were originally Etruscan tombs. Its treasures include a small museum of Jewish history in a sixteenth-century synagogue, the Museum of the Palazzo Orsini, and the Archeological Museum.

Sorano is perched on a cliff and dominated by a sixteenth-century fortress. Its livelihood now depends on a cooperative that creates some of the most delicious pecorino in Tuscany. Sovana is a partly abandoned village with a brick paved square. Around the village is an Etruscan necropolis, the Tufo City Archaeological Park that contains the Tomba della Sirena and the notable Tomba Ildebranda.

Saturnia, thirty minutes from Pitigliano, is a town named for the Roman god Saturn. Its attraction is the renowned thermal spa, Terme di Saturnia. The hot springs, flowing from the same spot for over three thousand years, gush into pools and Roman baths. Have lunch at I Due Cippi da Michele, or drive a little further to Da Caino, a cozy family restaurant located in the village of Montemerano.

Tuscan Notes ∾ SATURNIA

RESTAURANTS

I Due Cippi da Michele
Piazza Vittorio Veneto, 26/a
011-39-0564-601-074
Typical Maremman cuisine.

Ristorante Da Caino
Via della Chiesa, 4
58050 Montemerano
011-39-0564-602-187
www.dacaino.it
Outstanding foods and wines.

HOTELS

Hotel Terme di Saturnia
Via della Follonata
011-39-0564-600-111
www.termedisaturnia.it
Get away from it all.

Sorano Cheese Cooperative
Caseficio Sociale Cooperativo Sorano
Via La Fratta, 54
58010 Sorano
011-39-0564-633-002
Heavenly, fresh pecorino.

Monte Argentario

Porto Santo Stefano and Porto Ercole are fishing villages on Monte Argentario, connected to the coast by sandbars called *tomboli*. This is one of the best places to go snorkeling, as there are shipwrecks in the deep, clear waters. You can even take a ferry from Porto Santo Stefano to the island of Giglio.

In the early 1960s Monte Argentario became an insider secret among affluent Romans, and a new marina Cala Galera was built to accommodate their large yachts. One of the chicest resorts in Italy, Il Pellicano, is here. With lush gardens surrounding a beautiful pool and a private beach, it is a great place to relax in the most beautiful setting. The last time we were here the designer Valentino's sleek yacht was moored in the tranquil cove facing the hotel.

To continue a sybaritic lifestyle, stop at Alain Ducasse's L'Andana, located in Castiglione della Pescaia. The twelve-thousand-acre estate with olive orchards and vineyards originally belonged to the grand dukes of Tuscany. The pink nineteenth-century villa built for the last one, Leopold II, is now a luxurious hotel encircled by landscaped gardens and rooms designed with luxurious bathrooms. This is a good place to relax and savor legendary chef Ducasse's cuisine.

Tuscan Notes — MONTE ARGENTARIO CASTIGLIONE DELLA PESCAIA

HOTELS

Hotel Il Pellicano
Calli dei Santi
58018 Porto Ercole
011-39-0564-858-111
Unwind at this chic resort.

L'Andana
Località Badiola
58043 Castiglione della Pescaia
011-39-0564-944-321
www.andana.it
Luxurious resort and restaurant.

BELOW: The verdant landscape gardens of L'Andana—a luscious spot to just unwind and indulge.

Lucca

Often overlooked by many tourists, Lucca is one of the most delightful towns in Tuscany—a real treat for those who want to avoid the crush of crowds. Its history is long and illustrious.

It is the only city in Tuscany to resist the Florentines and has been stubbornly independent since the fourteenth century.

Napoleon Bonaparte's sister, Elisa, crowned the princess of Lucca and grand duchess of Tuscany, ruled Lucca from 1805 until 1813. A bit later, author and critic John Ruskin wrote that the town was so wonderfully preserved "in materials so incorruptible, that after six hundred years of sunshine and rain, a lancet could not be put between their joints."

Today, prim Lucca looks much like it might have back then. High brick battlements ensconce the city with five entrances. Narrow streets lead from one piazza to the next past Renaissance houses and medieval towers. No cars are allowed, so the town must be explored on foot or by bicycles, which you can rent.

The city's mercantile history—silk weavers, goldsmiths, bankers, and olive oil makers—is reflected in the name of its streets, squares, and charming shops, whose splendidly preserved facades reflect an earlier time. Some of the most elegant are on Via Fillungo where goldsmiths have been selling jewelry for over three hundred years. In the midst of this narrow street, through an archway, is the Piazza dell'Anfiteatro where a Roman forum once stood. Today boutiques and caffès line its circular rim. Wander through the back of the piazza and head over to the Palazzo Guinigi, to enjoy an amazing 360-degree view of Lucca and the countryside.

More than two dozen churches are to be found within Lucca's walls, some dating from the Middle Ages. The Duomo San Martino is known for its green and white marble exterior. Its Gothic interior contains *The Last Supper* by Tintoretto and a portrait of the *Madonna and Child* by Ghirlandaio. Another one of our favorite churches, the Romanesque San Frediano, houses a glazed terracotta roundel of the annunciation by Andrea della Robbia and the remains of Saint Zita, the patron saint of Lucca.

It's not possible to see it all in one day, but you can start with some special ones: the tiny Giacomo Puccini Museum (the composer was born in Lucca); the elegant Palazzo Pfanner with its formal garden; and the National Picture Gallery *(Pinacoteca Nazionale)* in the Palazzo Mansi with paintings by Paolo Veronese, Pontormo, and Tintoretto. On some days, you can watch demonstrations of the early Lucchese silk weaving done on old looms in the National Picture Gallery.

Lucca is famous for its culinary specialties. Its olive oil is said to be some of the best in Italy. The city's illustrious caffès and pastry shops have been offering Lucca's traditional sweets—such as the ring-shaped *buccellato di Lucca,* a cake made with fresh lemons and marsala wine—for well over one hundred years.

Several notable villas and gardens in the surrounding hills—summer palaces built between the sixteenth and eighteenth centuries—are open to the public (see Chapter Two). Garden lovers will also enjoy the Botanical Garden (Orto Botanico) and the Camellia Festival held every March (see www.camelielucchesia.it for information). On the third weekend of each month a much anticipated antiques market is in the Piazza San Martino.

This is a fascinating area of Tuscany to explore. The Garfagna region north of Lucca still remains relatively unspoiled. This remote area of pine forests and bubbling streams provides superb views of the snowy Apuane and Apennine mountains. Set in the steep hills are some attractive towns such as Barga.

Tuscan Notes ∽ LUCCA

RESTAURANTS
La Buca di Sant'Antonio
Via della Cervia, 1/3
011-39-0583-558-81
An old standby.

Ristorante La Mora
Via Sesto di Moriano, 1748
Sesto di Moriano
011-39-0583-406-402
www.ristorantelamora.it
Extraordinary food.

Trattoria da Giulio
Via delle Conce, 45
011-39-0583-55948
Big, boisterous, and good.

CAFFÈS
Buccellato Taddeucci
Piazza S. Michele, 34
011-39-0583-494-933
Typical Lucchese sweets.

Di Simo
Via Fillungo, 58
011-39-0583-496-234
anticocaffedisimo@tin.it
Delicious pastries since 1840.

ANTIQUES
Antico Anfiteatro
Piazza Anfiteatro, 29
011-39-0583-306-084
For the home.

Antica Ditta Giuseppe Pellegrini
Via Fillungo, 111-113
011-39-0583-491-305
Exquisite jewelry and silver.

Carli
Via Fillungo, 95
011-39-0583-491-119
The oldest fine goldsmith.

SHOPS
Antica Bottega di Prospero
Via S. Lucia, 13
www.bottegadiprospero.it
Forty different kinds of coffee.

Atelier Cas
Porto di Borgo
Corner Via Fillungo
011-39-0583-464-338
Home décor.

Cartoleria Paoli
Via Fillungo, 164
011-39-0583-491-435
Colorful art supplies.

Farmacia Massagli
Piazza S. Michele, 36
011-39-0583-496-067
Lucca's oldest pharmacy.

La Bottega di Mamma Rò
Piazza Anfiteatro, 4
011-39-0583-492-607
www.mammaro.com
Chic handmade linens.

La Grotta
Piazza Anfiteatro, 2
011-39-0583-467-595
Typical Lucchese food.

Le Ceramiche di Sugaro
Piazza Napoleone, 17
011-39-0583-464-557
www.sugaro.it
Pottery galore.

Le Matite
Piazza Citadella, 6
011-39-0583-312-834
Handmade stationery.

Le Sorelle in Lucca
Piazza Anfiteartro, 31
011-39-0583-486-31
marcomarconi_M@libero.it
Beautiful tabletops.

If you would like to see Tuscany in a more leisurely fashion, try a walking or bicycling tour.

Butterfield & Robinson
70 Bond Street
Toronto, Canada M5B 1X3
806-678-1147
www.butterfield.com

Cinghiale Cycling Tours
www.italian-connection.com

Insider's Italy
718-855-3878
www.insidersitaly.com

Italian Connection
11 Fairway Drive, 210 Edmonton,
Canada T6J 2W4
800-462-7911
www.italian-connection.com

Italian Dream Incorporated
Via Terraglio, 6-4
31021 Mogliano, Italy
011-39-041-593-6299
www.iditravel.com

VBT Bike Tours
614 Monkton Road
Bristol, VT 05443
800-245-3868
www.vbt.com

The Wayfarers
174 Bellevue Avenue
Newport, RI 02840
800-249-4620
www.thewayfarers.com

∾ ∾ ∾ ∾ ∾ ∾

A good map is a must if you don't want to miss anything—or get lost too often. We're partial to the excellent map of Tuscany from the Touring Club Italiano, which you can order from their website, www.touringclub.it.

A good guide book is essential.
We like the following:

Baedeker's Tuscany
ISBN 0749-519-975

Blue Guide Tuscany
ISBN 0393-323-455

Michelin Green Guide Tuscany
ISBN 2061-007-228

∾ ∾ ∾ ∾ ∾ ∾

For additional information, check out the websites of these two tourist boards:

Italian Government Tourist Board
630 Fifth Avenue, Suite 1565
New York, NY 10011
212-245-5618
www.italiantourism.com

Tuscan Tourist Board
Via Manzoni, 16
50121 Florence
011-39-055-233-20
www.turismo.toscana.it

LEFT: Some inviting old storefronts in Lucca.
BELOW: This beauty has been here for centuries.

EIGHT

Tuscany at Home

Where to Find the Sources

"Italia! Oh Italia! Thou who hast the fatal gift of beauty."

—Lord Byron

Years ago, it was an adventure to send a package home from Italy. Nowadays, when you find something that you can't live without that won't fit in your suitcase, it's not a problem. Most shops will happily ship your purchases and, in fact, most Italian cities now have postal service stores that make it easier than ever to bring Tuscany home.

But what about months after you've returned, when you get a yearning for the tasty flavors of Tuscany—golden olive oils, tangy vinegars, wheels of pecorino, fragrant salumi and sausages, crusty *biscotti*, not to mention the wonderful wines. And where will you get all the beautiful objects that you coveted—creamy bed linens, hammered silver serving pieces, ceramic pitchers, terracotta urns? We now live in a global economy and although you may not find every Tuscan nuance, you can certainly find more Italian merchandise in the United States than ever before—not to mention Italian-inspired designs that are copied all over the world.

In this chapter I have chosen stores and websites that reflect the Tuscan style. Some are favorite places I've shopped at for years, along with new additions. The Internet can be enormously helpful. You can now order delicacies from across the country that arrive shrink-wrapped at your doorstep within days.

I also love just wandering in New York City's Little Italy. I often stop to chat with Louis Di Palo, the owner of the landmark Italian food store Di Palo Fine Foods. For years, he's been happily recommending which Tuscan extra virgin olive oil to choose from his new shipment and unfailingly offers flaky samples of fresh cheeses to taste. If you can't actually *be* in Tuscany, this is the next best thing.

OPENING PICTURE: Antinori wines, Tignanello and Solaia grown in the Chianti Classico area south of Florence and Pian delle Vigne a Brunello, grown near Montalcino.
OVERLEAF LEFT: The sunny Tuscan kitchen at L'Andana and, right, a collection of vintage Tuscan maps and cards.
ABOVE: An old olive oil can sits behind bottles of some of the best olive oils being made today.

Food

What I look for when I'm buying Tuscan delicacies at home is fresh, fresh, fresh! Pecorino cheeses, pastas, and hard-to-find olive oils like Castello di Ama from Rogers International are just some of the wonderful things available. Here is a selection of sources, most of whom will ship.

A. G. Ferrari Foods
877-878-2783 (For a store near you)
www.agferrari.com

Arthur Avenue Deli
2344 Arthur Avenue
New York, NY 10408
718-295-5033
www.arthuravenue.com

Cantinetta Tra Vigne
1050 Charter Oak Avenue
St. Helena, CA 94574
707-963-8888

Copia
500 First Street
Napa, CA 94559
707-259-1600
www.copia.org

Dean & Deluca
Call for store locations
800-221-7714
www.deandeluca.com

Di Bruno Brothers
930 South 9th Street
Philadelphia, PA 19147
888-322-4337
www.dibruno.com

Di Palo Fine Foods
206 Grand Street
New York, NY 10002
212-226-1033

D'Italia
888-260-2192
www.ditalia.com

East 48th Street Market
2462 Jett Ferry Road
Dunwoody, GA 30338
770-392-1499

Eccentric Gourmet
3434 W. Anthem Way
Anthem, AZ 85086
623-551-4445
www.eccentricgourmet.com

Formaggio Kitchen
268 Shawmut Avenue
Boston, MA 02118
617-350-6996
www.formaggiokitchen.com

Grace's Marketplace
1237 Third Avenue
New York, NY 10021
212-737-0600
www.gracesmarketplace.com

Ideal Cheese Shop
942 First Avenue
New York, NY 10022
800-382-0109
www.idealcheese.com

IGourmet
877-446-8763
www.igourmet.com

Laurenzo's Italian Food & Wine Center
16385 W. Dixie Highway
N. Miami Beach, FL 33160
305-945-6382

Napa Valley Olive Co.
835 Charter Oak Avenue
St. Helena, CA 94574
707-963-4173

Rogers International
10 Dana Street
Portland, ME 04101
207-828-2000
www.rogersintl.com

Salumi
309 Third Avenue South
Seattle, WA 98104
877-223-0813
www.salumicuredmeats.com

Stonewall Kitchen
2 Stonewall Lane
York, ME 03909
207-351-2719
www.stonewallkitchen.com

Todaro Brothers
877-472-2767
www.todarobros.com

Williams-Sonoma
Call for store locations
877-812-6235
www.williamssonoma.com

Zingerman's
620 Phoenix Drive
Ann Arbor, MI 48108
888-636-8162
www.zingermans.com

Web Site Only

Gustiamo
718-860-2949
877-907-2525
www.gustiamo.com

This is the American offshoot of an Italian website that offers hard-to-find artisanal foods from Italy, and is one of Marcella Hazan's favorite sources. We order the extra virgin olive oil and red wine Chianti vinegar from Tenuta di Cafaggio, from here.

Wine

These stores have a good selection of Italian wines and a knowledgeable staff. You don't have to leave home if you check their websites or ask for a mail-order catalog—and, better still, they all ship anywhere in the United States.

All Seasons Wine Shop
1400 Lincoln Street
Calistoga, CA 94515
707-942-6828

Enoteca Wine Shop
1345 Lincoln Street
Calistoga, CA 94515
707-942-1117

Italian Wine Merchants
108 East 16th Street
New York, NY 10003
212-473-2323
www.italianwinemerchant.com

Morrell and Company
1 Rockefeller Plaza
New York, NY 10020
212-688-9370
www.morrellwinebar.com

Sherry-Lehmann
679 Madison Avenue
New York, NY 10021
212-838-7500
www.sherry-lehmann.com

Vino
121 East 27th Street
New York, NY 10016
212-725-6516
www.vinosite.com

Home and Garden

Here's a list of stores whose selection of tasteful merchandise for the home and the garden usually includes some wonderful Italian imports. There's bound to be something in stock that will give your home that Tuscan look, whether it's rustic country or sleek avant-garde. I've also included special places where you can find specific items, like ceramic tableware, linens, or even Italian seeds.

HOME FURNISHING AND ACCESSORIES

ABC Carpet and Home
888 Broadway
New York, NY 10003
212-473-3000
www.abchome.com

Bergdorf Goodman
754 Fifth Avenue
New York, NY 10019
800-588-1855
www.bergdorfgoodman.com

Ca'toga Galleria d'Arte
1206 Cedar Street
Calistoga, CA 94515
707-942-3900

Crate & Barrel
Call for store locations
800-967-6696
www.crateandbarrel.com

Eccola
326 North La Brea Avenue
Los Angeles, CA 90036
323-932-9922
www.eccola.com

Europe by Net
888-660-4870
www.europebynet.com

Hollyhock
817 Hilldale Avenue
West Hollywood, CA 90069
310-777-0100
www.hollyhockinc.com

Museum of Modern Art Design Store
44 West 53rd Street
New York, NY 10019
212-767-1050
www.momastore.org

Neiman Marcus
Call for store locations
888-888-4757
www.neimanmarcus.com

Pottery Barn
Call for store locations
888-779-5176
www.potterybarn.com

Sur La Table
Call for store locations
666-328-5412
www.surlatable.com

CERAMIC TABLEWARE

Fortunata
1413 Woodmont Lane, NW
Atlanta, GA 30318
404-351-1096

FABRICS

Brunschwig & Fils
979 Third Avenue
New York, NY 10022
212-838-7878
800-538-1880
To the trade only
www.brunschwig.com

Fortuny
979 Third Avenue
New York, NY 10022
212-753-7153
To the trade only
www.fortuny.com

Old World Weavers
979 Third Avenue
New York, NY 10022
212-752-9000
To the trade only
www.old-world-weavers.com

Scalamandré
222 East 59th Street
New York, NY 10022
212-980-3888
To the trade only
www.scalamandre.com

The Silk Trading Co.
Call for store locations
888-745-5302
www.silktrading.com

FLOOR AND WALL TILES

Bisazza Mosaico
43 Greene Street
New York, NY 10013
212-334-7130
www.bisazzausa.com

Country Floors
15 East 16th Street
New York, NY 10003
212-627-8300
www.countryfloors.com

FURNITURE

B & B Italia
150 East 58th Street
New York, NY 10155
800-872-1697
www.bebitalia.it

Conran Shop
407 East 59th Street
New York, NY 10022
866-755-9079
www.conran.com

De La Espada
33 Greene Street
New York, NY 10013
212-625-1039
www.delaespada.com

Domain
Call for store locations
800-436-6246
www.domainhome.com

GARDEN FURNITURE AND STATUARY

Barbara Israel
296 Mt. Holly Road
Katonah, NY 10536
914-744-6281
www.bi-gardenantiques.com

Chilstone
Victoria Park
Fordcombe Road
Langton Green, Kent TN3 0RE
011-44-(0)-189-274-0866
www.chilstone.com

Florentine Craftsmen
46-24 28th Street
Long Island City, NY 11101
718-937-7632
www.florentinecraftsmen.com

KITCHENWARE

Bridge Kitchenware
711 Third Avenue
New York, NY 10017
212-688-4220
www.bridgekitchenware.com

LEMON TREES

Spring Hill Nurseries
110 West Elm Street
Tipp City, OH 45371
513-354-1509
www.springhillnursery.com

LINENS FOR BED AND TABLE

Cittadini Linens
1673 Northern Boulevard
Manhasset, NY 11030
516-365-7114
or
171 East 67th Street
New York, NY 10021
212-756-8781
By appointment

Frette
799 Madison Avenue
New York, NY 10021
212-988-5221
www.frette.com

Pratesi
829 Madison Avenue
New York, NY 10021
212-288-2315
www.pratesi.com

Pucci
701 Fifth Avenue
New York, NY 10022
212-230-1135
www.emiliopucci.com

PAINT

Janovic Plaza
Call for store locations
800-772-4381
www.janovic.com

SEEDS

Seeds from Italy
PO Box 149
Winchester, MA 01890
781-721-5904
www.growitalian.com

SILVER ACCESSORIES

Buccellati
Call for store locations
800-223-7885
www.buccellati.com

Bulgari
730 Fifth Avenue
New York, NY 10019
212-315-9000
www.bulgari.com

SOAPS

Lafco
285 Lafayette Street
New York, NY 10012
212-925-0001
800-362-3677
www.lafcony.com

TERRACOTTA GARDEN POTS

Smith & Hawken
Call for store locations
800-940-1170
www.smithandhawken.com

White Flower Farm
P.O. Box 50, Route 63
Litchfield, CT 06759
800-503-9624
www.whiteflowerfarm.com

Organizations and Societies

One of the ways you can learn more about Tuscany and do some good at the same time is to join organizations of like-minded people interested in preserving the cultural, artistic, and agrarian traditions of this glorious region. The cradle of the Renaissance, with its extraordinary artistic patrimony, needs support from all of us around the world to preserve and maintain it.

"Nowhere in Italy—and perhaps even in the entire world—is the act of looking at art more rewarding than in Florence. Nowhere else is one captivated by a wistful Botticelli smile, impressed by the graceful dignity of Donatello's bronze *David* and moved by Michelangelo's provocative *Slaves* twisting restlessly in their marble prisons." This statement by Friends of Florence founder Contessa Simonetta Brandolini d'Adda explains why she started the foundation in 1998. An American living in Florence, she called upon her American friends to join with prominent Florentines to help protect the city's cultural legacy. The foundation was created to encourage individuals to participate in the restoration and preservation of the innumerable artistic and cultural treasures located in Tuscany, and in particular Florence.

Their first project was the cleaning and restoration of the marble statues in Florence's Loggia della Signoria, the city's main square and gathering place. It was just the first of many. The organization has recently finished the program of diaganostic analysis of Michelangelo's *David* and is embarking on the restoration of an entire room of the Uffizi Gallery, the Sala della Niobe. If you are a fan of Florence, become a Friend of Florence as well.

Friends of Florence
4545 W Street, NW
Washington, DC 20007
202-333-3705/8228
www.friendsofflorence.org
or
Via Ugo Foscolo, 72
50124 Florence, Italy
011-39-055-223-064

Two other worthy organizations are:
Friends of FAI
Allesandra Pellegrini
Via Broletto, 43
20121 Milan, Italy
011-39-0271-2141
www.fondoambiente.it

World Monuments Fund
95 Madison Avenue
New York, NY 10016
646-424-9594
www.wmf.org

The Slow Food movement was started in the 1980s by an Italian journalist (see Chapter Three). It has grown by leaps and bounds and now has branches in forty-five countries worldwide, with an office in the United States that you can contact if you would like more information. Oldways, founded in 1990, promotes healthy, traditional, and sustainable food choices and has coordinating programs tied in with Italy.

Slow Food
20 Jay Street, #313
Brooklyn, NY 10013
718-260-8000
www.slowfoodusa.org

Oldways Preservation and Exchange Trust
266 Beacon Street
Boston, MA 02116
617-421-5500
www.oldwayspt.org

Suggested Reading

If you are traveling to Tuscany or simply want to savor the richness of the region, the following is a selection of favorites that I've enjoyed over the years. Some are out of print but can be found on websites such as Amazon and Bookfinder. And if you're a mystery buff, don't miss Magdalen Nabb's atmospheric books set in Florence.

Acton, Harold. The Last Medici. London: Macmillan, 1980.

Anderson, Burton. Treasures of the Italian Table. New York: William Morrow, 1994.

Barzini, Luigi. The Italians. New York: Atheneum, 1985.

Beevor, Kinta. A Tuscan Childhood. New York: Vintage, 2000.

Bell Italia. Historic Houses and Gardens Open to the Public in Italy. Milan: Giorgio Mondadori, 1996.

Bentley, James. The Most Beautiful Villages of Tuscany. London: Thames & Hudson, 1997.

Borsook, Eve. The Companion Guide to Florence. London: Collins, 1973.

Capalbo, Carla. The Food Lover's Companion to Tuscany. San Francisco: Chronicle Books, 1998.

Cardini, Franco. Tuscany, Landscape, History, Art. Florence: Scala, 2003.

Castelvetro, Giacomo. The Fruit, Herbs, and Vegetables of Italy. London: Viking, 1989.

Clarke, Ethne and Raffaello Bencini. The Gardens of Tuscany. London: Weidenfield & Nicolson, 1990.

David, Elizabeth. Italian Food. New York: Harper & Row, 1987.

De'Medici, Lorenza. Florentines, A Tuscan Feast. New York: Random House, 1992.

------------. The Renaissance of Italian Gardens. London: Pavilion, 1990.

D'Epiro, Peter and Mary Desmond Pinkowish. Sprezzatura: 5o Ways Italian Genius Shaped the World. New York: Anchor Books, 2001.

Forster, E.M. A Room with a View. New York: Bantam, 1988.

Hazan, Marcella. The Classic Italian Cookbook. New York: Alfred A. Knopf, 1983.

Hazan, Victor. Italian Wine. New York: Alfred A. Knopf, 1982.

Hibbert, Christopher. The House of Medici: Its Rise and Fall. New York: Perennial, 1999.

Hobhouse, Penelope. Gardens of Italy. London: Mitchell Beazley, 1998.

James, Henry. Italian Hours. New York: Penguin Classics, 1995.

Jenkins, Nancy Harmon. Flavors of Tuscany. New York: Broadway, 1998.

Johnson, Hugh. Tuscany and Its Wine. San Francisco: Chronicle, 2000.

King, Ross. Brunelleschi's Dome. New York: Penguin, 2001.

Macadam, Alta. Americans in Florence. Florence: Giunti Editore, 2003.

Masson, Georgina. Italian Gardens. Suffolk: Antique Collector's Club, 1987.

McCarthy, Mary. The Stones of Florence. New York: Harcourt Brace Jovanovich, 1959.

Moorehead, Caroline. Iris Origo: Marchesa of Val D'Orcia. London: John Murray, 2000.

Morelli, Laura. Made in Italy. New York: Universe Publishing, 2003.

Murray, Peter. The Architecture of the Italian Renaissance. New York: Schocken Books, 1986.

Origo, Iris. War in Val D'Orcia. Boston: David R. Godine, 2002.

------------------. Images & Shadows, Part of a Life. Jaffrey, NH: David R. Godine, 1999.

Origo, Benedetta, Laurie Olin, John Dixon Hunt, and Morna Livingston. La Foce. Philadelphia: University of Pennsylvania Press, 2001.

Praz, Mario. An Illustrated History of Interior Decoration. New York: Thames & Hudson, 1982.

Romer, Elizabeth. The Tuscan Year. New York: Atheneum, 1985.

Ross, Janet. Leaves from Our Tuscan Kitchen. New York: Ballantine, 1987.

Russell, Vivian. Edith Wharton's Italian Gardens. New York: Bullfinch Press, 1997.

Sabino, Catherine and Angelo Tondini. Italian Style. New York: Clarkson N. Potter, 1985.

Schinz, Marina. Visions of Paradise. New York: Stewart, Tabori & Chang, 1985.

Simon, Kate. Italy, The Places in Between. New York: Harper & Row, 1970.

Spender, Matthew. Within Tuscany. London: Penguin Group, 1992.

Wells, Patricia. Trattoria. New York: William Morrow, 1993.

Willinger, Faith. Red, White and Greens. New York: Harper Collins, 1996.

Wirtz, Rolf. Art & Architecture Florence. New York: Barnes & Noble, 2000.

Wright, Sarah Bird. Edith Wharton Abroad. New York: St. Martin's Press, 1995.

∽ ∽ ∽ ∽ ∽ ∽

There are also many magazines on Italy. The ones I'm enjoying now are FMR, *a gorgeous publication known for its stunning art direction;* La Cucina Italiana, *which is known for its homey recipes; and* Gambero Rosso, *an insider's guide to Italy's top wines, travel, and food. If you want to subscribe contact:*

Speedimpex USA
800-969-1258
www.speedimpex.com

Veronelli, the company that does the well-respected Gold Guides on restaurants, wines, olive oils, and hotels also publishes a magazine called Veronelli EV.
Unfortunately, it is only published in Italian, which is a good reason to start brushing up on yours. You can subscribe on their website:

www.Veronelli.com

*"Dreaming through the noble Tuscan landscape . . .
I feel that life is altogether bounteous and good,
lovable, manageable, sweet."*

—Barbara Grizzuti Harrison

In the heart of ev

he is born, what

and tastes, there

which is Italian...